The Complete Nigerian

by

Peter Enahoro

MALTHOUSE PRESS LTD

©Peter Enahoro
First Published 1992
ISBN 978 2601 73 — X

Malthouse Press Limited
8, Amore Street,
Off Toyin Street, Ikeja.
P.O. Box 8917, Lagos.

Editorial Suite
12th Floor, Western House,
8 - 10 Broad Street, Lagos.

Associated Company
Malthouse Publishing (UK) Limited,
19A Paradise Street,
Oxford, OX1 1LD UK.

By the same Author

How to be a Nigerian (1966)
You Gotta Cry to Laugh (1972)

Acknowledgements

'Sad' Sam Amuka; Chief W.C. Onykwere;
Popo Akinyanju; Kanmi Isola-Osobu. . . .
Simply, thank you for being there.

I DEDICATE THIS BOOK

To My Sons
Alexander and Mark . . . .
who are too young to know
the truth I speak;

To My Wife
Susanne. . . .
who must know by now what she
let herself in for when she married a Nigerian;

To My Brother
Christian. . . .
without whose affectionate help
my re-entry into Nigeria would have
been harder still.

The Complete Nigerian

A self-confessed tale-bearer's guide book to the doings and misdoings of the Nigerian adult male and female.

by Peter Enahoro

Contents

Prologue

The following is a story that must be told.

The book in your hand is not a warmed-up corpse of *How To Be A Nigerian*. It is a sequel no doubt; a companion perhaps; but not a cosmetic regeneration, like a rejuvenated mama energised with sillicone implants to put new life into the old bag.

You can tell already I'm not over-fond of *How To Be A Nigerian*.

I have loathed that book. It was never a finished work and I have always resented its success. Here's why.

In the abridged narrative of its origins published in the *Foreword*, I recount how the idea for the book was given to me by a German journalist I thought was a friend.

Lutz Herold was introduced to me by Dr Karl Wand, Press Counsellor at the West German Embassy in Lagos. Karl and his sexy Swedish wife, Dagmar were easily the most popular foreign diplomatic couple in Nigeria at the time, trusted by all and honoured with chieftaincy titles.

Lutz was a spy.

I did not know it and I did not suspect it. He was arrested during the OAU Summit in Accra, in 1965. Even after he was jailed 40 years by Kwame Nkrumah's regime in Ghana for 'misimprison of treason,' I did not believe it. I thought Nkrumah was up to his anti-West tricks and had picked on my friend for maximum publicity, at a time when the eyes of the world were on Ghana.

I went about Accra trying to rally a protest among foreign journalists covering the Summit, even suggesting that we staged a mass evacuation of the conference.

Another German journalist brought me to my senses. Fritz Lüdecke was the Nairobi-based correspondent of the German news agency, DPA. He took me aside and cautioned, 'Don't get involved in something you know nothing about.'

Lutz Herold was released from jail following the 24 February, 1966 overthrow of Nkrumah. At first he returned to Europe where the foul agent divorced his loyal wife on the grounds that she had not done enough to secure his freedom.

Sometime later that year, I was in Cologne and working for Radio Deutsche Welle when, one evening, the secretary of the head of the Africa-English department summoned me to receive a visitor. I had not expected to see Lutz Herold ever again. But there he was beaming the emotional smile of a long lost brother. I embraced the lout warmly and invited him to a celebratory drink.

Afterwards my nominal boss, Konstanz Schmölder, who had been the Labour Attache at the Germany Embassy in Lagos at the time I was introduced to Lutz, said accusingly to me, 'You were with that man, Lutz Herold.'

'Oh, yes,' I enthused, 'Isn't it wonderful to see him again!'

'I don't want to see him ever again in this office,' Schmölder rasped in a tone he had never used to me before.

I took offence, of course. 'What have you against my friend?' I asked with some heat.

'Lutz Herold is a spy for South Africa,' Schmölder told me.

So Nkrumah had been right and I had been a fool.

Lutz Herold confirmed his allegiance when he

retired to live in apartheid South Africa. I don't know if he's alive or dead. I don't care.

I've never forgiven him.

I've never forgiven myself either for falling sucker to his blandishments, and I've disrelished *How To Be A Nigerian*, ever since for its association with a treacherous friend.

Besides, the book should never have been published in its form. The facts are these:

Egged on by the aforementioned Lutz Herold, I took time off work to put down some thoughts on the lines he'd suggested. Perhaps too hastily, I gave the raw efforts to Felix Iwerebon, an old school-mate, for evaluation. Felix was the Nigeria representative of Longmans, a United Kingdom publishing company. He was apparently impressed and forwarded the collection to London.

After what seemed an age, London replied saying that in the opinion of the editors Nigerians were not ready for the kind of humour.

My brother Michael had recently returned from study in Britain. I defensively sought his opinion. The manuscript soon had Michael making sounds as though clearing his throat. It was a good sign. Among my family we shyly clear the throat to signal high praise for each other.

Michael and I plotted that I should test the Nigerian temperament by publishing selected excerpts in the *Daily Times*. The reader response was no surprise to us.

And so it came to pass that when I left Nigeria in August 1966, I was still in the process of putting flesh to the raw materials, as well as constructing new chapters.

It is now twenty-five years and more since the *Daily Times* surprised me with its compilation of the unfinished work. I have grudgingly accepted the acclaim that *How To Be A Nigerian* received. It has never ceased to amaze me. Think how absurd a music composer must feel whose fame is based upon his unfinished symphony.

At last, however, I can put *How To Be . . . etc.* behind me.

A new generation has grown up since the premature outing of that malnutritioned godson of the deceitful Herold. The generation about which I wrote in 1966 has produced grandchildren. In the intervening period, we have fought and settled a civil war and enjoyed the doubtful benefits of an oil-boom economy. These events have had their dramatic impacts on our culture and national character. Also in the intervening period, our lives have been mainly directed by a military political class and our sense of humour, our appreciations of our surroundings, have been affected thereby.

From all this a new Nigerian has emerged bearing his lot with another kind of vigour, fortitude, boisterousness, inventiveness, enrichment and organized chaos. In 1966, I could write, 'The search for the Nigerian is in progress.' A quarter of a century later, I can say with certainty that the discovery has been made.

The Complete Nigerian is here.

Peter Enahoro
Lagos, 1992.

1

The Name

FIRST, let us pause for a bit of history. The name *Nigeria*, how did we get it?

There is no earthly reason why our country should be called Nigeria. It might as well have been called Songhai, after a defunct empire which at least incorporated parts of our country. It is true one would have been highly inconvenienced going around telling people, 'I'm a Songhaian,' or 'I'm a Songhairi.' I can just hear the Chinese: 'You Chongkai?' Even so, history would have been on our side.

Consider the discarded name, *Gold Coast*. Kwame Nkrumah didn't feel a fraud when he pinched *Ghana* from the history books. Every school boy knows that the Ghana of yore was in today's Guinea and that in those days Guinea stretched all the way across the Sahara just west

1

of Sudan, which was Ethiopia when Ethiopia was Abyssinia.

And then take a careful look at the Republic of Benin. Quite shameless what they've done to themselves! There was only one Benin and it was continually at war with Dahomey, which was the country of today's self-styled Beninois. Then the modern Dahomeans lost their heads and proudly took a name that used to make their ancestors spit.

If we were really pushed for a name we could have chosen to call our country *HIFEKINIYETU* which you will recognize from its association with HausaIboFulaniEdoKanuriItsekiriNupeIjaw-YorubaEfikTivUrhobo. Why ever not? What's so special about *Nigeria?*

History would have us believe that 'Lady' Mary Lugard, the common law wife of Nigeria's first Governor-General rose from behind her desk one morning and gave the name to Frederick Lugard. Just like that. What nonsense.

I have a more plausible story.

It is not the name she invented that really matters; it is when, how, where and why she made it up. At what precise moment did the bolt of serendipity strike the Lady Lugard in the head? After hearing my story you can decide for yourself whether the answer reveals something

2

sordid or whether it is a fable you can tell in front of your children.

For myself, I am satisfied that our country's name derived from one woman's wily interference in the affairs of state, because her lover had been ignoring her.

This was what happened:

Before she took his name, Mrs Lugard worked as Frederick Lugard's secretary. Which tells us that sexual harassment in the work place did not begin with the Complete Nigerian. This is not to say that old Fred had a roving eye. He wore a severe monocle which made it difficult for his eye to rove. As a matter of fact, it took a while before his eye rested appreciatively upon the woman behind the notepad and pencil. And if the truth be told the old boy was rather past it by the time he refused to make an honest woman of the old girl.

As may be expected, this had its problem for the alleged Mrs Lugard who was really Miss Mary Shaw.

To begin with, Frederick Lugard was an imperialist agent of the worst kind: a man full of noble intents and of himself. He had achieved success in Uganda and had arrived in the Niger Area of West Africa determined to further his notoriety.

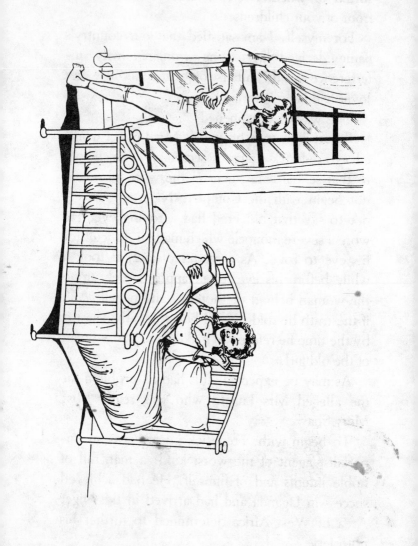

Perhaps understandably, he was not content to be master over a territory known only as the 'Niger Area.' He worried that his image and glorious imperialist career might be impaired. This fear occupied his mind morning, noon and night; especially at night.

The woman who liked to pass herself off as Mrs Lugard was driven to distraction.

Early one morning, their faithful servant of many years, Hamzat stood outside their bedroom door. He carried in his hands a bundle of three-month-old copies of *The Times* which had newly arrived by rail, ship and horse-back from London.

Hamzat was about to knock on the door when he heard his master's raised voice. He stopped in his tracks. In order to apprise himself of what was going on, he bent low and peeped through the keyhole, eavesdropping.

Frederick Lugard was standing by the window dressed only in his long-johns. He was scratching himself. Mrs Lugard lay half-propped up in bed, hair tussled, notebook and pencil in hand from force of habit.

Hamzat heard his master say to his mistress, 'It's this damned heat.'

Mrs Lugard replied sceptically, 'It's been three months . . . you've simply lost interest in me, admit it!'

There was a puzzled look on the old rascal's face and Hamzat saw him gaze at his mistress with a certain interest. 'That long?' he mused faintly.

Mrs Lugard nodded slowly, several times.

'If only you could lump the damned lot of them together and give them a proper common name,' she said, brightening up a little. 'Hausa, Fulani, Kanuri, Ibo, Yoruba — the lot. Something like. . .' her voice trailed away.

'You'd have the natives warring over a common name,' Frederick Lugard muttered feebly. 'If it is Yoruba the Ibos will not want it.'

Mrs Lugard was busy doodling on the notepad. The intensity registered in her face told Hamzat, whose aching back was killing him at key-hole that, 'Madam' was furious.

'Well let's have something neutral, something they can't beef about; something absolutely meaningless; something that has no historical or traditional connotations. They'd be mad to quarrel over a name that merely described the area. . .' She stopped so abruptly Hamzat thought she'd lost her voice.

'There!' she cried triumphantly. 'I have it!' She threw the notepad and pencil in the air, raising her arms. 'By God, I have it! *Nigeria* — from *Niger-Area*. The Americans have given

6

the Grain Coast people *Liberia* from *liberty*. Well, why ever not *Nigeria?* With a name like that you could even ask Whitehall to let you amalgamate the North and South Protectorates. Who else would they make. . . who else could they make, Governor-General? *Sir* Frederick,' she sneered. 'You should be *Lord* Lugard!'

'Say that again,' murmured her husband softly.

'*Lord* Lugard!'

'No, no. The name. Of the country.'

'*Nigeria.*'

Lugard lowered himself to sit on the bed beside his live-in girlfriend. 'Darling, say it once more,' he whispered choking with emotion.

'*Nigeria.* And it is entirely my very own little invention.' Mrs Lugard breathed sexily. 'And you don't have to marry me.'

'Oh darling, you are divine,' said Frederick Lugard.

'Oh my darling, welcome back,' said Miss Shaw fluttering her eyelashes invitingly.

Frederick Lugard embraced his 'wife'. Mrs Lugard embraced her 'husband'. Whereupon, Hamzat delicately withdrew from the key-hole.

Later that day, he reported everything he had heard to Alkali Jumat, who in turn told it all to the district head.

As time went by the story arrived in Rumukourushi, where the noted oraculist Calestus Okonkwo Emelum adapted it into his incantations. This was inherited by succeeding generations of Emelum oraculists who kept it strictly within the family oral traditions.

But a sly British colonial officer named T.R. Batten, who was a clandestine client of a juju-priest, picked up the gist of the incantation and put it down on paper.

He meant to include it in his *History of Nigeria*, but the Colonial Office forbade him to do so dismissing it as tittle-tattle. Instead, British propagandists laid down the official version so that history will always show what a caring, clever old bird the late Mrs Lugard was.

Until now my version has remained a secret known only to Boniface Cletus Chukwudi Emelum, a herbalist; his brother, Aloysius Ubaldus Obediah Emelum, a spare-parts dealer; and their cousin Celestine Innocent Odumegwu-Njiribeako, the catechist of St. Saviour's Oracle of the Lord-in-Heaven Church of Christ-the-King, Rumukourushi.

It is to that God-fearing gentleman I owe the privilege of this exclusive tale. It was he who told it to me when I discovered the Christian preacher conducting fertility rites on his day off from church service.

From him we have obtained the truth that Nigeria was given its name by a frustrated paramour after a depressing night during which she lay beside her beau and failed to arouse his libido.

We now know also that when the passion returned, Frederick Lugard immortalized his happiness by decreeing the name 'Nigeria' for all eternity. He imposed it on an astonishing conglomerate of native emirates, kingdoms, principalities, chiefdoms and village republics, all of which had no say in the matter.

2

We the People

NIGERIANS are Ibos, Yorubas, Hausas, Fulanis, Tivs, Nupes, and Kanuris but you may also call them Nigerians.

When a Nigerian really wants to go hoity-toity with you, he will ask you, 'Do you know where I come from?'

What he means is, do you know he is Edo, Ibibio, Efik, Urhobo, Itsekiri, Ijaw or any one of the eighty other ethnic varieties, and that he only happens to be a Nigerian?

Nigeria is a country, it is not a nation, and that is what he is telling you.

Yet there is such a person as the Complete Nigerian. He is a child of expediency.

An astute politician once said, 'Nigeria is a geographical expression.' Not any more. Nigeria is an expression, period.

It is this expression that unites the Ibos.

11

For three heart-breaking years, the Ibos fought bravely, nay suicidally, to separate themselves from Nigeria. An irony of that struggle was the mutual distrust which highlighted the identities and the deep suspicions between 'Midwest-Ibos,' 'Nnewi-Ibos' 'Onitsha-Ibos,' and 'Abriba-Ibos.'

The Nnewi-Ibos, the others said, were greedy and grasping. Onitsha-Ibos were scorned as arrogant and treacherous. The Midwest-Ibos boasted they were the best soldiers; and the poor Abriba-Ibos were unjustly accused of depleting Biafran battalions to enrich their starved dinner tables.

Without Nigeria the Yorubas would be at each other's throats.

At the height of the Western Region crisis in the mid-1960s, when Yoruba was pitched against Yoruba, combatants would precede the exchange of mayhem with the loaded inquiry, 'Are you Ijebu or are you human?'

Without Nigeria the Ishans would resume their guerrilla warfares against the Benin monarchy.

The Itsekiris and the Urhobos would burn down Warri town because they could not agree who owned it.

The Tivs would return to the security of their

ancient plateau redoubts daring the Hausas to come up and fight.

The Fulani jihadists might even resume their epic horse-back crusade towards the sea in search of a holier cause than the quest for oil-money.

And the riverine Ijaws would sooner trade with the head-hunters of Papua New Guinea than sell smoked fish to their Isoko neighbours.

Nobody quite knows how many Nigerians there are. Some say 88.5 million; others say 110 million. It depends on who has conducted the count and for what purpose.

Nigerians speak more than 500 dialects, drawing a latter-day suspicion that when the Tower of Babel collapsed its survivors were scattered over the surface of Nigeria.

3

Are You Not a Nigerian?

FOREIGNERS in our midst must be puzzled by the frequency with which they hear one Nigerian ask another, *Are you not a Nigerian?*

Does this mean that we Nigerians cannot distinguish one another from the Pygmies of Ubangi-Shari? Far from it.

Are you not a Nigerian? is a peculiarly Nigerian idiom.

It is a rhetorical question meant to deceive, to put you off your guard.

It is an angry retort.

It is an excuse for misbehaviour.

It is an idiom to seal a bargain.

Let us say you are a Nigerian arriving at Murtala Mohammed International Airport in Lagos, on an overnight flight from mid-winter Europe. You are clad in thick wool. The time is 7 a.m. and the stifling humidity is already beginning to steam the body.

14

Predictably, the air-conditioning is not functioning.

You have been standing in a queue for what seems a decade; finally, you are before the Immigration desk, perspiring. You address the Immigration Officer, a Complete Nigerian, trying to make small talk:

'I see the air-conditioning has failed again.

The Complete Nigerian Immigration Officer, magisterial in manner behind the desk, gazes long and hard into your passport as though checking your criminal record. This takes some twenty minutes. You know at once you have hit a raw nerve, especially when he begins flipping through all the pages of the passport. Which takes all of five minutes.

If he is in a lousy mood and does not wish to talk to anyone that morning, especially to big-mouthed passengers like you, he will put his stamp on your passport and hand it back to you without comment. Do not hang about.

However, he may be willing to converse. in which case, you have asked for it. He does not like your comment about the air-conditioning! He does not like people from abroad, especially those Nigerians who enjoy the means and privilege to see foreign places telling him the air-conditioning is not functioning. He knows it is faulty. He knows the air-conditioning at Murtala Mohammed Airport only works two days a year. But he is not in charge of the air-conditioning. You should know that. Why blame him? It is early in the morning and you want to spoil his day. He does not like your attitude. In fact, he doesn't like you. So, he does not put his mark on your passport: he hammers it into it. Then, ever so slowly, he goes through it again, page after page. At last, without looking up from the document, he asks you gruffly, *Are you not a Nigerian?*

This is in reply to the observation you made a half hour ago about the state of the air-conditioning and it is his idiom for, 'piss off!'

Do not hang about.

*   *   *   *   *   *

You are driving a flashy car and you are unlucky to have to ask your way. It would be perfectly reasonable for you to shout your inquiry through the open car window because of the din of car horns blaring behind you, ordering you to move on.

You would soon know if the policeman directing the traffic is a Complete Nigerian.

'Drive on' he growls at you. 'You're holding up the traffic!'

But you are a Complete Nigerian yourself and Complete Nigerians do not take nonsense from traffic policemen. At any rate not in broad daylight. So you sit tight and ask him in plain English, 'Which is the way to Ademola Street?'

It would have been helpful if you had driven a little further on, parked the car properly making sure you are not impeding the traffic, and walked back to ask the way. But why should you? *Are you not a Nigerian?*

In any case such civilized behaviour has been overtaken by events. Several cars have taken it upon themselves to engage the openings around you and the policeman, to make their escape. Because everyone is trying to perform the same miracle at the same time the traffic jam has built into a giant spaghetti snarl-up. Where is the policeman meanwhile?

Long ago he stopped directing the traffic and walked over to deal with you. It would have been so much easier for him to say, 'Ademola Street is second left, first right. Have a nice day.' Instead, he says, 'Park the car!'

'What for?'

'I say park the car! I want to see your papers.'

He plants himself in front of your car, waves others to stop and guides you to the roadside.

The traffic-jam is doing nicely without his help, with kilometre-long queues of honking cars in every direction.

The trouble is you do not have your papers on you. *Are you not a Nigerian?*

'*Oga*', the policeman says triumphantly, 'you do not have your licence, no insurance certificate.'

'I've got them at home,' you trumpet equally triumphantly. 'I can bring them to the station.'

But the policeman is a shrewd fellow; he tells you, 'I can charge you with obstructing the traffic.' You know that despite his tone, his manner suggests he has no intention to do so.

So, you say candidly, 'I don't have the time to make court appearances. What can we do?'

You are a Nigerian!

The policeman relaxes his mood, a faint smile crosses his face as he says to you. '*Oga*, you are a Nigerian, not so?'

This is a variant for, *Are you not a Nigerian?* and asked in a friendly manner. It is idiom for, 'Make me an offer. . .'

*   *   *   *   *   *   *   *

Suppose you wish to purchase an item of merchandise and you cannot reach agreement with

"Are you not a Nigerian?"

the seller after half an hour of haggling? You might say to your adversary, 'I could have bought this in Cotonou at half your price.'

With a straight face he tells you. *'Oga*, this is Nigeria.'

You reply, 'So?'

'You should bargain,' the Complete Nigerian urges you ingratiatingly.

'I don't have time to bargain!' you thunder.

The Complete Nigerian is unruffled.

'Massa' he says graciously, *Are you not a Nigerian?'*

This puts you off your guard.

*   *   *   *   *   *   *   *

There is probably no time when the question is more loaded than when asked under conditions of stress.

For example, one Nigerian seeks a favour from another.

Ahmed Musa is Nupe and proud of it. He is to appear before an interview panel and he has learned that it is headed by one Okon Bassey Okon, from Akwa Ibom State.

Ahmed Musa has heard of Akwa Ibom State but he has never met anyone from Akwa Ibom State. Ahmed Musa does not give a damn for

Akwa Ibom State. If he spent three score and twenty more years on this planet, nothing would induce Ahmed Musa to go out of his way to discover Akwa Ibom State. As far as Ahmed Musa is concerned Akwa Ibom could be a foreign state.

But he must prepare for the interview in the proper Nigerian way. He must seek to influence the panel before his scheduled appearance.

Ahmed Musa goes to see his uncle Alhaji Shehu Ahmed, the family's Complete Nigerian.

Alhaji Shehu Ahmed has resided in Lagos for the past fifteen years during which he cultivated the acquaintance of 'Southerners'.

'The chairman is from Akwa Ibom,' Ahmed Musa informs his uncle disconsolately.

But his uncle is optimistic. He knows one Etim Ukot Etim whose origins are in Akwa Ibom.

Although Etim Ukot Etim does not know Okon Bassey Okon personally, he confidently assures Alhaji Shehu Ahmed, 'Don't worry, we are from the same place. I will talk to him.'

Alhaji Shehu Ahmed is encouraged but not altogether convinced. So, to buy his nephew a double insurance at the start, he says casually, 'We are all Nigerians.'

Etim Ukot Etim is satisfied that Alhaji Shehu Ahmed is a good egg.

21

'Alhaji, how long have we known each other? Five, six years?'

'More. Seven and half years, to be exact.'

'Seven and a half long years! Time flies. As you say, we are all Nigerians.'

'Yes,' muses Alhaji Shehu, 'that is why I came to see you. The chairman is from your country.'

This does not stun Etim Ukot Etim. Not even an ignorant Nigerian would use the word 'tribe'

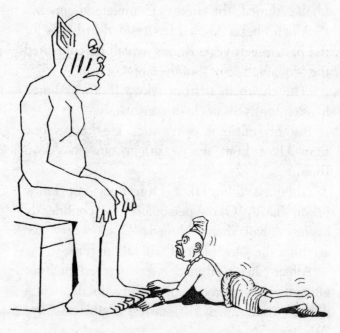

"I am thy Lord thy tribe!"

in these circumstances. Etim Ukot Etim acknowledges the distinction by saying, 'Yes, the chairman is from my country,' adding meaningfully, however, 'but he's a Nigerian. He will want something. . .'

Now Alhaji Shehu Ahmed has to show whether he is truly a Complete Nigerian or whether he is just a long-winded hustler trying to profit from an indifferent familiarity of seven and a half years' duration.

He seems to be both, for he answers evasively, 'I do not know what to say. I'm entirely in your hands.'

Etim Ukot Etim enlightens him readily. 'Alhaji,' he says softly, *Are You Not a Nigerian?*

They have understood each other.

4

The Curse

IN Nigeria, a man without tribal consciousness is a man without religion. He exists, but he is like a Christian without the Church; a Moslem without Mecca.

Tribal awareness is as inherently native to the psyche of the Complete Nigerian as whisky to the Scot.

Insofar as the Japanese without his *kimono* is colourless, so also is the Complete Nigerian minus his tribal kit without lustre.

The history of the United States would be incomplete without the gun. Likewise, the record of our political development would be fragmented without the stories of our inter-tribal violence.

The Englishman relishes his dullness when he steers the conversation to his native weather. Only talk about his royal family makes him even more dull. Similarly, the Complete Nigerian bore cannot resist a passionate discourse on the evils of tribalism, at which time he becomes as tiresome as the Englishman and his weather chat.

As the opium transports the Chinaman into a seventh heaven so does tribe intoxicate the idle Complete Nigerian. One day it may kill him; meanwhile, he is hooked on it.

Foreigners snigger and titter at our preoccupation with tribal awareness and rivalries. They say it is a self-induced scourge and that if we would only stop talking about it we would soon achieve national harmony. If they only knew!

The fact is that Nigerian tribal sensibility is a curse from God; it is long past ordinary human weakness. This is a fact of history.

When the European colonialists seized our lands and willy-nilly unloaded their protection upon us (for our own good, remember?) they abolished our ancient nationalities with a stroke of the quilt. In order to maintain their supremacy, they slandered our kingdoms, our principalities and our empires by defaming them as mere tribal societies.

This strategy of conquest by disparagement had been earlier formulated by the slave-traders who devised the plan so that they would not have to pay wages to the labourers they needed

for the plantation farms in America. They handed the blueprints of their tricks to the missionaries who in turn justified their cultural im-
positions by equating our nationalisms with anti-
Christ primitiveness. In a trice we were required
to surrender not only our existing national identities to a new, supra-nationality, but along with
that, also to give up our customs and traditions.
Today, if two Nigerians from the same ethnic
group converse in what is called their 'tribal
language,' in the presence of a third Nigerian
from a different ethnic group, they will be con-
demned for subverting Nigerian national unity.
'These tribalists,' you will hear the cry, 'they
won't speak English!'

Archbishop Desmond Tutu of Johannesburg,
a high-ranking South African man of God, has
given evidence of how the missionary conquest
was accomplished.

'When the White man came,' he said, 'he
gave us the Bible and said, "Let us pray." When
we opened our eyes, we had the Bible, and he
had the land.'

Archbishop Tutu did not go on to say what
followed, but I have it on good authority that
God was extremely displeased. For was it not
His deliberate plan which created the Ibos, the
Hausas, the Edos, the Efiks and all the other na-
tions? And was it not He who gave the peoples

of those nations their separate and distinct national tongues, the same as He gave the English people the wisdom to pilfer their language from the Greeks, the Romans, the Germans, the Dutch, the French, not to mention the Hindus and even the native American Indian from whom he stole 'okay?'

And has anyone labelled the Northern Irish Republican separatists of the so-called United Kingdom, 'tribal separatists?' Or, deprecated the mettle of the Kurds of Iran similarly? Never!

Is it not so that, instead, their tribal emotions are recognized internationally as 'nationalist susceptibilities,' whereas our similar sentiments are disdained as the rather barbarian instincts of peoples trapped in the unrefined mentalities of ancient ethnicisms?

Is it not the case that we hear only of 'Scottish nationalism' but never 'Scottish tribalism?'

And why should the Ibo, the Yoruba and the Kanuri, for example, who in their individual aggregates number in several millions be labelled 'tribes,' but the Welsh, a mere handful millions are accorded the status of nationhood?

Is it not so that what we call 'tribalism' today is the strong pull of a nostalgic throw-back to our original nationalisms, and are you surprised that God should be angry that we, for whom He

"Thou art cursed. . . I gave thee Nations but thou dare'st call them Tribes!"

went into all the trouble to create nations, joined the foreign interlopers in belittling His creative genius as mere 'tribes' when it is obvious they are nations?

Hence I say to you that God put the curse of tribe on us, in revenge for our readiness to ape the White man's derogation of His achievements for us.

Yet such is the infinite mercy of God that despite His wrath tribe can be good for you.

For instance, when properly manipulated your tribal origins can earn you that job for which you are not qualified. When it is finely tuned, it can deny your rival the promotion he so richly deserves.

Tribe can enrich you beyond your means. It can lose your business competitor a contract.

It wins elections.

It either protects against, or it provokes, the successful military *coup d'etat*.

Tribe is Mafia.

In its creature form it is a brotherhood, as intuitive as the instincts of jumping goats. Let me explain.

If you herd ten goats before a fence and one of them suddenly jumps over it, the others will automatically follow suit and leap over the fence, although there is no rational incentive for them to do so. That is tribe.

'Tribe is like kerosene,' a friend said to me. 'A drop of it spreads wide.'

If you employ a Complete Nigerian to head your domestic staff and you give him the freedom to fill the remaining vacancies, you have made a mistake; unless you wish to fill your household with members of his tribe. They will follow in his wake as surely as a herd of galloping sheep follows the lead of the beast at the head of the formation.

In a colourful way, tribe is superstition.

A friend of mine had lived in London for donkey's years and had become so thoroughly Anglophile in his tastes and manner even newer hands at Buckingham Palace used to ring him up for advice on how to set the Queen's dinner table.

Yet this same man, this very same Anglophile Nigerian friend of mine, who had lived so long in England people used to stop him in the streets to ask his autograph so they could show it to their grandchildren, that same individual received a daring threat from the supreme executive of his tribe's cultural association. His hands were shaking as he showed me the letter written on the headed paper of the 'Ezobo Descandants' Union Joint Action Committee.' In the left-hand corner of the page was the legend: 'Motto: One Fatherland.'

'Dear Brother,' the letter read, 'this is the third and final notice to you to send your contribution towards the town union fund for the church building. I do not wish to repeat all I said in previous letters, but I must remind you that wherever you are in this world, home is home.

'Second, I must intimate you with the knowledge that at the last meeting of the entire union held in the palace of our father, His Highness . . . the sacred oath was sworn in the name of our forefather that when those who fail to donate to the church fund join their ancestors, the entire town should boycott their funeral rites.

'As our people say, the dead cannot bury the dead for the dead. If you do not reply to our appeal it will mean we are all dead to you . . . Yours in Christ and the service of the fatherland.'

'Ignore it,' I said pretending to be unimpressed.

'Of course,' said my thoroughly Anglicized Nigerian, breaking into a cold sweat.

Two days later, when he was struck down with a high fever we decided we were playing with fire. The evil hand of tribe reaches far. We decided he should send a generous donation to his tribal union and immediately he did so he felt better.

I fully understood. You can't put strange powers past some tribes!

I myself know of a tribe who when its people reach a certain age can transform themselves into fairies in the dead of night. They gather as giant fireflies on the tallest *iroko* tree in the market-place every seventh day to drink human blood.

I heard all this from a trusty maid when I was seven years old and I still spin round three times to cast away the evil spell every time I encounter a member of the tribe in the streets. Even now, well into adulthood, I dare not mention the name of the terrible tribe. Its people are so versed in *juju*, so powerful in witchcraft they can murder a man by remote control, by transmitting poison invisibly over a great distance.

The fear of being ostracized is a powerful fetish invoked to service the tribal brotherhood. That is why your recruiting domestic staffer will tell you that all those people he has engaged in your service are his brothers and that he has brought them on board for your own sake. He will lie in his teeth and tell you he can only trust his fellow tribesmen with your possessions.

After they have robbed you blind, he will tell you it is because 'they are not from my hometown.' Why did he tell you they were his brothers?

'*Massa*,' the Complete Nigerian fellow will tell you without batting an eye, 'we are from the same place.'

Do not even attempt to argue the logic with him, for you cannot defeat a Nigerian on matters of his tribe.

* * * * * * * * *

Tribe is the common denominator by which we Nigerians evaluate the worth of each other.

If two Nigerians are discussing a third Nigerian and they cannot remember his name, it would be perfectly adequate for one of them to say, 'You should know the man I'm talking about . . . you know . . . that Yoruba man.'

If the absent person is held in good favour, every effort will be strained to identify him by his name and the conversation may even be held in abeyance while a thorough search is made. The good have names, the bad are tribesmen.

Therefore, if on the other hand, he is not held in good esteem, nothing further need be said about his personal identity. With the mere mention of his tribe, a mental identikit of the absentee will roll across the vision on the basis that all members of a tribe share the same awful characteristics; the same objectionable social, political and economic outlooks. The same bad breath, bad teeth and the same unspeakable moral deviations.

The parents' association at a village school physically attacked a teacher, to discourage him exercising a sexual attraction among their children, some of whom were coming home swooning over his good looks. He had not committed any offence as yet, the beating was just a warning.

Rumour was rife in the community that his people worshipped mermaids who rewarded the men of the tribe with extraordinarily handsome features and gave the women a sexiness that simply went *oomph!* All this was confirmed by the school's head teacher, a very tall and stately spinster whose limited facial hairs gave her away to be a woman.

Tribe is so pervasive it filters into the churches, where congregations have been known to split over the appointment of a new parish priest because he came from the wrong tribe.

In former times our leaders rallied their political forces with the exhortation that our unity must be in our diversity. In fact 'unity in diversity' was a euphemism for 'unity in adversity.' Every tribal group felt it was not getting its 'fair share of the national cake,' as we used to say. 'Unity in diversity' was therefore a clarion call for tribal exclusiveness in the face of the adversity of having to share a nation with other tribes!

Three generations of civilian and military political leaders tried to pretend that tribal considerations did not matter in their planning, but the survival of the Nigerian state did not begin to look plausible until states were created to conform to tribal and clan boundaries.

Our late and lamented National Anthem of the First Republic paid due homage to tribe with the words: 'Though tribe and tongue may differ . . . In brotherhood we stand, Nigerians all . . .'

An overzealous military regime killed it off alleging that it perpetuated tribal sentiments. Yet the same administration instituted a policy popularized as 'reflecting the federal character,' by which federal appointments and admissions to federal schools and colleges were allocated to mirror what was elegantly called, 'the national geographical spread.'

That classy phrase was a chic disguise for a blatant policy designed to pander to tribal prejudice.

Since campaigners say we should ban all mention of tribe altogether, I for one must beg for time.

Such people are the careless talkers who would like to make it socially unacceptable for a man to identify himself proudly as an 'Ijesha tribal violinist.' They want to encourage a purveyor of that harsh and unrhythmic trash called *apala* to pass himself off as a 'Nigerian musician,' and thus ensnare our patriotism into defending the thing.

Apala is not music. It is nerve-jarring, cacophonous, grating, dissonant bedlam, usually accompanied by a shrieking soloist who has had an unsuccessful throat operation. I shall cease to be a Nigerian the day the appallingly loud and unpleasant sound is recommended for inclusion in our national musical consciousness.

Only the Yoruba people are entitled to understand what an *apala* drummer is fussing over when he starts beating an inflated leather pouch hanging loose in the region of his intimate person, with chopsticks spirited from a Chinese take-away.

I make this other threat:

If it ever became the fate of this nation that the wind instruments played by the trumpeters and flautists at Argungu Fishing Festivals should travel anywhere further than their place of origin, and if it should ever become obligatory that we welcome the orchestrated din they raise as exemplars of pan-Nigerian national musical repertoire, I shall resume a life of exile!

There is such a thing as good tribal music for those who wish to hear it. They will find it among my Ishan people, 1,300 ft. up on the Kukuruku Hills plateau.

Music, for me, is when an Ishan songstress springs to her feet bopping, weaving, swaying, working herself into a frenzy as she embarks with complete abandon upon a creatively off-key rendition of her own improvised lyrics, hitting the high notes with a clarity that would shatter glass.

Music is when a euphoric Ishan audience tries to rouse itself to support her efforts and surprisingly agile septuagenarians leap to their feet and manage to hold the last note of the chorus despite a long evening at the bottle.

Music is when a choir of Ishan husbands playing home-made musical instruments, including empty beer bottles, are seeing themselves home from a rousing night out, and their voices filter through your open window.

That is what good tribal music should be - joy from deep in the soul of an Ishan man after a solid helping of pounded-yam.

I haven't lived amongst them all my life but yet the magic calls me to surrender. And that, my friend, is the curse of tribe.

5

The Art of Grumbling

OURS was once a nation of excellent grumblers.

We grumbled in anger; we grumbled in mirth. We grumbled about nothing at all, and we grumbled just about everything. It was ridiculous. We were terrible grumblers.

Nigerian grumbling was a bizarre eccentricity which others tried to emulate without success.

Once upon a time we had a large colony of Lebanese merchants in Nigeria. They were natural grumblers themselves, but they were not good enough. Despite their reputation as monotonous grumblers, and in spite of their long association with us, many left Nigeria to go and help destroy their beautiful country. They should have learned to grumble boastfully but act less decisively like we used to. It may have sapped their energy but it would have saved their country from the wreckage they inflicted on her.

At the height of our grumblesome years, we grumbled with gusto, and constantly filled the air with full-blooded oaths, which were heard coherently above the hubbub of market noises.

'My father, I'm dead!' you would hear someone declare. Or, if the declarant was not dead, 'I'm lost for ever!'

Such declarations were preludes to the most ferocious grumbles which, however, petered out as nothing.

Nigerians were so good at grumbling foreign employers said in admiration that a Nigerian could grumble all day long and still have the energy to get some urgent work done two days late.

British imperialists especially appreciated this strength of character. They said it took plenty of grit to engage in marathon political grumbles about your colonial master and then have the decency at the end of the day not to burn down his house. For years the British Press described Nigerians as 'level-headed.' That explained why British colonialism did not hasten out of Nigeria. Today we like to say. 'We fought for independence.' It is not a particularly accurate choice of words. We struggled for our independence, to be sure; but fight?

The truth was we argued and quarrelled freely amongst ourselves most of the time, although we

grumbled about the British and even, sometimes, to the British! But we did not break loose on a rampage of armed rebellion like some countries which shall remain nameless.

Yet our tactics worked. Eventually the British became so fed up with us, they handed us independence 'on a platter of gold,' exactly as Dr Nnamdi Azikiwe, our first President, who was a great orator and a frontline architect of our anticolonial struggle, so richly put it.

For a brief spell our market *mammies* were the most visible exponents of our penchant for grumbling.

It was no skin off her nose when an overweight market *mammy*, a mother of ten, grumbled for hours on end about promiscuity among young people. Nor did it trouble her to moan about lazy council health workers, though she herself presided over the fetid odours in a stall harbouring a colony of flies.

During the world-wide feminist crusades of the 1960s, our most famous women journalists imitatively grumbled and became household names. You could not open a newspaper without some feminine harridan moaning fancifully about women's liberation. Then one after the other, they wrote themselves into a *cul-de-sac* of unreasonableness, and got sucked into a well-earned oblivion.

Their departure coincided with the end of an era. For soon Nigerians were never again to be good and hearty grumblers. Indeed, only a relatively few Nigerians are grumblers at all these days. The Complete Nigerian does not grumble. He gossips instead.

The decline and fall of the merciless grumbler began when we lost our sense of proportion. We grumbled ourselves into a civil war and it was because we took our grumbling un-characteristically seriously. It was weird, for previously we knew where to draw the line bet-ween Nigerian bombast and a dangerous and damaging grumble.

Our mistake started with our trade unions. They specialized in grumbling.

When at last the government of the First Republic had heard enough complaints from the union leaders, it grudgingly awarded pay rises across the board, having first itself grumbled about Communist infiltration of the trades union movement.

The salary increases had the landlords and commercial interests grumbling that they were left out of the show. How were they expected to survive when everyone around them was getting paid higher, new wages? So, the landlords and businesses took away the increases from the workers by arbitrarily raising rents and retail prices.

Our wizard 'economists', myriads of them (i.e. virtually anyone with or without a university degree who published an opinion in a newspaper) grumbled expertly that the government should impose statutory rents and prices control, to deal with the profiteers.

Which was rather ignorant of them because the *nouveau riche* were the government themselves, and that kind of thing causes trouble.

For instance, our Minister of Finance was so well off that, on one occasion, to show us his opulence, he tied the ends of a spectacular thirty-foot loin-cloth to the necks of two page boys, to dramatize his entry into the House of Representatives on Budget Day.

Grumbling - not your dull, inarticulate, humdrum murmurs, or the rumbling grunts, the cringing whinings of the lily-livered or fainthearted - I mean serious grumbles, of the type which blows down houses and maims limbs -became highly popular. So, the government of the day decided to win the elections without the votes of the *hoi polloi* who it blamed for the troubles. It arranged to have the elections rigged instead.

Technically this was a simpler and far more exciting electoral process than appealing to the masses, or getting heckled by ignoramuses, or even organizing your supporters to queue all day at polling stations, in blazing sunshine.

The results gave Nigerian grumblers something to really get their teeth into rather than waffling on and on about commonplace issues as was the custom previously. Unfortunately it was a novel experience and we could not handle it.

The opposition political parties registered unrestricted grumbles.

Even the President of the Republic went on the radio to grumble.

The government became agitated, got off its backside and fought back. Its hack writers were commissioned to pen vitriolic grumbles.

Eventually everyone was grumbling so noisily we lost our dignity and went to war to silence one another.

Even so, we may never have fought the Civil War if the 'Northerners' and the Ibos had grumbled and like everyone else, had sought to let the matter rest at that. After all, the escalation towards the Civil War accelerated in earnest when Chukwuemeka Odumegwu-Ojukwu grumbled that Yakubu Gowon was the junior in rank and should not be Head of State.

Gowon was so livid he grumbled back immediately.

Both sides swore they wished to end the war but each grumbled that the other party was unreasonable.

Then Ojukwu fled and the Biafrans grumbled that there was nothing more to fight about.

Did the Civil War last as long as it did because the person of Chukwuemeka Odumegwu-Ojukwu got in the way? historians are already asking, grumbling.

After the Civil War came a new mood, a new understanding of our surroundings; a new awareness of what we had accidentally let ourselves into. Enter, the Complete Nigerian.

No longer could Nigerians grumble openly and without fear or favour as in the previous times which quickly became remote from our political senses.

The succession of military governments meant that Nigerians had to devise new techniques and invent other methods to compensate for the loss of the open-hearted grumble.

Thus came the age of the Great Unfinished Statement, otherwise known as Cursing Your Luck. It is the new weapon wielded by the Complete Nigerian in place of the guileless grumbles of yesteryears.

Because Nigerians could no longer grumble at large, to their heart's content, the Complete Nigerian became devastatingly sly and evasive with rumour-mongering, which is the current culture.

Oladimeji is a successful stockfish retailer. He was at school with Rufus, a street-wise barber, and a Complete Nigerian.

One day, Rufus sees his old classmate driving past in a beat up Datsun car, a thing he bought cheap as a retired taxi. On the evidence of that jalopy and nothing more, Rufus decides that Oladimeji is doing well in life.

There was a time in our culture when Rufus would have enjoyed Oladimeji's success by attaching himself vicariously to his friend's ascendancy.

He would have gone about boasting to everyone that they were at school together; he would have told massive fibs about the things they did as children; then, he would have cursed his own fate, grumbled about a bad decision in choosing the barber's trade, blamed the government for not supplying free salons to barbers, blamed God for his tribe; and, with that, he would have generally had a good day. Or, in the alternative, he would have gone home to beat his wife, which was the same thing.

But times have changed.

So, when Rufus runs into Mathias, a fellow-sufferer on the lower rungs of the achievements ladder, he does not enjoy a good grumble as in times past.

'You look vexed,' says Mathias observing the scowl on Rufus's countenance. 'How's life?'

'Life? What life? In Nigeria?' queries Rufus.

'I know,' says Mathias, 'there is no life left to live in Nigeria.'

'Wonders shall never end,' Rufus says morosely.

'What can a man do?' adds Mathias in support.

This prompts Rufus to elaborate. 'Remember Oladimeji?'

'Ola the Cat?'

'Ola the Cat! You musn't call him that any more.'

'We were classmates.'

'Yes, we were. But I saw him a few minutes ago.' Rufus shakes his head sadly. 'To think it was the same Ola.'

'He didn't greet you?'

'Me? Little me?'

'Ola saw you and didn't stop to say, hello?'

'Why should he? He almost had me spattered all over with mud as he drove past in his new

47

car! Do you know what car it was? Ah! Nigeria!'

'Come on, stop pulling my leg. How can a man selling old fish in Balogun Market afford to by a new car?'

'Well, sit where you are and keep asking questions. This is Nigeria!'

They part company.

On his way back to his bicycle repairs shed, Mathias stops to call on Baby-Face Ajasco, another old school pal. Ajasco is a saxophone player. He is also a pretty prodigious lyricist who has written protest lines such as,

Tell me, who rules Nigeria?
Contractors rule Nigeria.
Tell me, who rules Nigeria?
Armed robbers and pen robbers rule Nigeria.

'I am sorry for Nigeria,' Mathias says to Ajasco without ceremony. 'I've just seen Rufus and what he had to tell me about Oladimeji surprised me. Remember Ola the Cat?'

'Di Ola'meji,' Ajasco sings. 'How's the Cat these days?'

'Don't ask me. I won't have you say you heard it first from my mouth.'

'Heard what?'

'Brother, these are not the days when one says things. . .'

'Doesn't he sell stockfish anymore?'

'Who knows for sure what people do these days? You and I slave away. Do you know what car he was driving? Ah. . . Nigeria!'

As Mathias takes leave of Baby-Face Ajasco, he gives the message: 'By the way, I've not said anything to you. Oladi's uncle's wife is the second cousin of the aunt of my sister's daughter's husband's half brother. So you see he is my relative. You understand? I don't want trouble from the family.'

Mathias is hardly out of sight when Ajasco leaves home for the beer parlour where he holds a credit account with Mama Calabar, a vast and matronly she-been proprietress in whose unlicensed premises early revellers go to warm up before setting off to drink seriously.

'Ajasco Baba!' Shola Odunsko calls out from a darkened corner of the parlour. Odunsko describes himself as a 'petty trader'. His establishment is a tin shack on the lower side of Olowogbowo area of Central Lagos, which supplies a nest of smugglers' warehouses as well as a distribution centre for stolen goods.

'What's up?' Odunsko asks as Ajasco settles down to a beer.

'I've chewed granite,' says Ajasco employing a newspeak Nigerian idiom. It means, 'times are hard'.

'Business is bad?' This from Odunsko.

'Some people are doing well. I've just been talking to Matty. I couldn't believe my ears. Oladimeji is driving a brand new car. Do you know what car it was? Ah. . . Nigeria!'

'No way! How can he afford it?' queries Odunsko.

'Nigeria has changed. Who cares about morality any more?'

Odunsko volunteers an opinion: 'I wonder if it is his cousin who's servicing him. He is a Minister. Oladi must have got a contract.'

'Is it for me to say?' muses Ajasco, surely a rhetorical question which actually supports Odunsko's suspicions.

Later that evening, Odunsko is chatting to Femi Ikpe, an investigative journalist who lives in rented accommodation in the same compound. Odunsko casually mentions that a friend had confided to him that an unnamed political powerhouse had awarded a fantastic contract to his mistress's half-brother (Remember the innocent Oladimeji?).

The story has moved so fast and changed so much in character Oladimeji is now a mystery man ('name withheld', as Nigerian newspapers like to say) and he has become a multi-millionaire.

He forms the subject of an editorial comment the following morning in the *People's Daily Echo:*

> As our fearless investigative reporter, Femi Ikpe popularly known in journalistic circles as 'First with The News' reports on the Front Page of this paper today, corruption in public life has reached such proportions that a man posing as a stockfish retailer is driving around town in a Rolls-Royce. . .'

Whatever happened to the ancient Datsun?

The *Echo* comment has the entire nation spellbound and speculating manfully. Before long Oladimeji becomes a political leader who has set up a front in Oyingbo Market where, the rumour now says, he is secretly printing counterfeit naira notes with the connivance of the government, and using them to buy stockfish from Norway. He is 'a Nigerian businessman who has a private aircraft!'

'Anything can happen in Nigeria,' the editor of the *Echo* maintains when challenged to identify his 'rich millionaire.'

Ten months after that day when Oladimeji unknowingly drove past Rufus and inadvertently triggered the rumpus, Nigerians are scarcely surprised when the voice of a previously unknown military officer tells them in a dawn broadcast that the Armed Forces have staged a *coup d'etat*, 'in order to arrest the trend of corruption, nepotism, financial mismanagement, political unrests. . . to save our great nation from further disasters.'

There are several arrests, and Oladimeji is 'netted', to borrow another favourite Nigerian journalese, in the general swoop. Inquiries galore are announced; in particular inquiries into the importation of stockfish, which is suspended until further notice.

'Our country needs discipline,' the new Information Minister tells the Press. In the same breath, he says, 'Freedom of the Press is guaranteed by the new government.' This is ominous.

Cheers go up and all seems well.

Eight weeks later, Okobi Diopa, who made a fortune bringing advanced electronic equipment into Nigeria during the severest import controls and who has two adjoining stalls in Alaba International Market, which is situated off the road between Lagos and Cotonou, rolls into town with an eighty-foot wide satellite dish. He deposits the monstrosity on the site of a house still under construction, in an area of Ikeja known to local wags as Cocaine Avenue.

'Who owns that?' Femi 'First-With-The-News' Ikpe asks the taxi driver returning him home from a binge one night.

'That?' asks the taxi driver who has not the foggiest idea. 'They say it belongs to General Yan Ga.'

The next morning, from the *People's Daily Echo* comes the following: 'Unconfirmed reports that senior military personnel are buying up Millionaires' Row at Ikeja, Lagos, have led to widespread speculations about corruption. . .'

That night, at the People's Chapel, a seedy night club where Baby Face Ajasco is held in reverence, the saxophonist/lyricist belts out a new popular number:

> 'Nothing changes, nothing changes
> In Nigeria
> Only names and the titles
> Of our leaders'.

As so often with our special characteristics, Nigerian rumour-mongering has no equal.

Ours is not a cheap variety of the village gossip with its backsliding whispers across a garden fence, nor is it the blathering chinwags of idle housewives.

Our rumour-mongering has style. It is quietly, effectively malicious and supremely masked.

6

Etiquette

THE man who fabricated the saying, 'Time and tide wait for no man' must have led a sheltered life. He never met the Complete Nigerian. Otherwise, he would have known that throughout history time has always stood around and respectfully waited for the Complete Nigerian.

I have no information about the coming and going of tides, but it would hardly surprise me to learn that the Complete Nigerian has found a way around that as well.

We have a thing called 'Nigerian Time' which has no respect for man-made horological devices. Nigerian time is embedded in the subconscious of the Complete Nigerian. It is an invention of Mother Nature and has been around since time began. Its charm is that its accuracy is regulated by individual whims and ego.

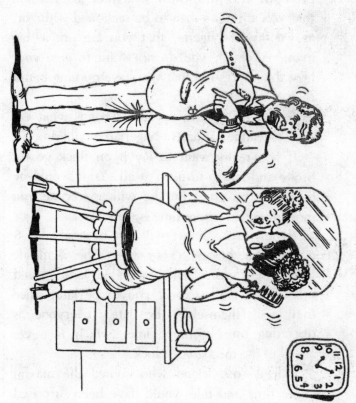

"Hurry up! Dinner is at 8!"

If a Complete Nigerian invites you to dinner for 8 p.m. do not disgrace yourself by arriving promptly at 8 p.m. Such behaviour will tell him that you are not a man to be reckoned with; or, as we say in Nigeria, that you are not a 'big man.' After all, you do not want to give your host the impression that you have nothing better to do.

Be careful to turn up late. That is what the self-respecting Complete Nigerian would do.

If you really want to lay it on thick go for broke and fail to turn up at all. Your would-be host may be upset but he will appreciate you more as a man whose time is valuable.

At any rate, dinner will not be ready for 8 p.m. Your hostess, your host, the domestic help, the children, the extended family, and other guests, all, expect you to be late, since they will themselves be late. Everyone is operating on Nigerian Time, which is never ahead of the mechanical clock.

Indeed, our friend who coined the maxim about time and tide would have been surprised to find to what extent the Complete Nigerian is highly sensitive about his arrivals and departures being regulated by the clock. He even carries this resentment unto death. Ask any officiating priest or Imam how often Complete Nigerians who have passed on are late to arrive at the stated time of their own funeral.

If you are one of those strange Nigerians who keep faith with the mechanical clock and you arrive for a dinner appointment on schedule, your Complete Nigerian host will think you are greedy. At least he will regard you with suspicion.

'Hasn't he got any food in his own house?' he will whisper in self-defence to his harassed wife, who is yet to have her hair washed. The woman may even round on him behind your back for having, as they say, 'useless friends.'

* * * * * * * * *

It is good manners not to appear to be carrying a sharp appetite when invited to dinner. Therefore, refuse everything at the first offer.

'Will you have a drink?'

'I'm not sure I should. I had a couple of whiskies before I left home.' (This is a lie. You've not had a beer all week for lack of the necessary wherewithal).

'Oh, go on, have another.'

'All right then, just a tiny bit.'

After this interlude pour yourself a full glass of

57

the fiery stuff. Your host will mark you down as well-mannered.

Every time your glass is empty you may say at the top of your voice, 'Where's the beverage, man? I thought you offered me a drink!' This is guaranteed to break up the house. You are enjoying yourself hugely.

By the time dinner is served you would think you were invited for breakfast. Be bold and say so to your host. The Complete Nigerian has the right frame of mind for alcohol-induced wit. So, pour yourself another brimful glass of whisky, what the hell! Make a rumbustious night of it; a proper Nigerian dinner party consists as much of heady fluids as of hefty comestibles.

Remember this (if you can still remember a thing) do not lunge at the table the moment dinner is announced.

Pace yourself; hold back; hesitate.

Remember (try anyway) to exhibit no interest whatever in the whiff drifting from the kitchen. Tell your hostess you are too drunk to eat anything. This may be true but she will think you are a Complete Nigerian showing excellent breeding.

Wait until she says wearily, 'You must eat something in my house for a change.' Then, protest that you've always eaten in her house, and proceed to prove it.

Heap more food on your plate than you would expect to eat in a week. This shows that you trust the cook.

Having tucked in fully to your stomach's content make sure there is enough left on the plate to feed a nation of cockroaches. If you clean up altogether, you will be thought gluttonous. Besides, you must assist in creating the wastage that will show the dustmen what a generous party giver your host is.

The classy Complete Nigerian does not only boast of the variety and quantity of chow he serves at his bash, he is equally lyrical about the left-overs to be thrown away. During the course of the evening he will repeatedly draw the attention of his guests to the excess food on the table with comments such as, 'Look at all this food, who'll eat it?'

When invited to a party take all your friends along, but remember to forget to warn your host. Showing off in this way is a rudimentary courtesy of the Complete Nigerian. Take liberties with your host, it would please him to tell your mutual friends you thought so highly of him you gave no notice you were bringing your friends to his home.

'Odunfemi?' he will boast. 'Of course I know him. He doesn't have to inform me he's coming to my house. Even when he brings his friends without forewarning me.'

This is every day one-upmanship, however.

The ultimate snobbery is when you say of a friend, 'I can do whatever I please in his house.'

You are not bragging and your wife is not overjoyed. Next time, she knows, the roles will be reversed and your pal will use your home for activities you cannot announce on the radio. His wife will not be overjoyed.

* * * * * * * * * *

It used to be thought good manners in our country to belch loudly and clearly at the end of a hearty meal. It was a compliment to your host and it told him you'd enjoyed yourself to the point of being sick on his carpet, if he had one.

If you are a traditionalist Complete Nigerian acquainted with this custom, go ahead and please yourself. The world is full of the strangest etiquettes.

Among the mountain people of Afghanistan for instance, they break wind to thank the host for a delicious meal.

Imagine the atmosphere, not to mention the sounds, as several windy guests choose to express their appreciations simultaneously, as they depart *en masse*. Can any meaningful conversations take place, and does anyone hear the 'goodbyes' being said, above the roars?

* * * * * * * * *

The Complete Nigerian is shy about certain things. Among them is paying back borrowed money.

In the Western societies of Europe and America, the borrower is adjudged vulnerable to exploitation and he is therefore elaborately protected by the law. In Nigeria, the risk lies with the lender.

The onus rests on him to behave delicately and with civility. A breach of confidentiality instantly brands him a tale-bearer and potential usurer. It is the one endeavour on which you can take advantage of the Complete Nigerian, with impugnity.

For example, if you are a distant cousin and you have borrowed money from your Complete Nigerian kin, you can safely write off the debt on his behalf, as a bad debt. He dares not press you for it lest he be denounced by the wider family as insensitive and selfish.

Remember that ours was once a sharing society and it is still not the done thing to ask a member of your family, even of the extended family, to refund a loan. That is about the meanest thing a Complete Nigerian can be guilty of in the eyes of society, tantamount to demanding money with menaces.

There are, however, times when your relation is so strained for cash himself, he may damn the consequences and arrive unannounced, on your doorstep. Do not give him a chance to take the initiative.

As soon as you sight him coming up the footpath, dash out of the house with a joyous shriek and take hold of him by the neck, in a friendly gesture. Then shower him with a welter of brotherly greetings.

You: 'Welcome!'

He (struggling to disengage from the death-grip): 'Thank you, thank you.'

You (warmly): 'How's everything?'

He (half-suffocated): 'Everything's fine.'

You (half carrying and half shoving him towards the door): 'Come in, come in.'

Once inside the house, steer him away from the most comfortable chair, and sit him on the footstool. Then, without a break in your stride, summon the entire household.

'Mama Wole! Mama Subu! Where are these women? Where are the children? Saibu!

Omole! Josiah! Ebenezer!' Turning to the visitor you moan to him, 'If you only know what I have to go through with this family every day. A man has two wives and yet he can't get attention when his kinsman comes to see how they are; whether they are in good health; whether they are fed. Seiko! Where's that daytime watchman? Seiko!'

Seiko appears.

'Sah?'

'Summon Mama Wole and Mama Subu. Tell the children to come and say hello to their uncle.'

When the family is assembled, stare your cousin Joseph hard in the eyes and dare him to introduce the unpleasant matter of your debt. No Complete Nigerian, even though his heart was hewn from granite, would brave it.

As you see him off, say casually, as though in afterthought, 'By the way, about that little matter between us, I'm working on it.'

He will give you a look fit to kill, but you are surrounded by mutual blood relations and no Complete Nigerian would have the nerve to defy the intimidation of a pedigree line-up such as arrayed before him. Invoke the genealogical bond between you two with a prayer. This should remind him that blood is thicker than water, although water was not the reason he came to see you:

'May the spirits of our ancestors go with you. May we never endure public humiliation in our family. May you never be tempted to steal from the church fund. May our secrets never become public knowledge. May you never wet your wife's bed. And may you grow the grey hairs of old age in your nostrils, and live long, far into old age, to continue to guard over us.'

The chances are good that before he takes his final leave of you, Cousin Joseph will make a cash gift to the children. Tradition says he ought to.

Protest vigorously while at the same time noting the pocket into which your eldest son has put the gift.

Make another animated statement: 'I can't let you do that. You've done enough for us already.'

While this charade is being played out Cousin Joseph is consulting his wrist-watch. His visit has been useless and he can't get away quickly enough.

Meanwhile, your eldest son has been fooling around with Cousin Joseph's largess, showing it to his brothers.

'Give me that!' you snap. 'Do you think money grows on trees? Do you know how hard Uncle Joseph has to work for it?'

You seize the funds and place it in your own pocket. Cousin Joseph knew all along it would end up there.

'When do we see you again? I hope it will be soon.' Thus you.

'Not bloody likely,' Cousin Joseph says to himself. The wretched man is fit to be taken away in an ambulance. But he smiles wanly and says, 'Soon. God bring you joy.'

And you respond, 'Ah, Cousin Joseph, as long as you are alive God must smile on me!'

*   *   *   *   *   *   *   *   *

Another trick is the Neighbourhood Appeal strategy.

Allow your cousin time to settle into a chair. He would be committing an abominable *faux pas* were he to plunge straight into the matter of his mission. However bitterly he may feel towards you, convention dictates that he must wait patiently for the right moment to introduce the debt issue. Fill the interval with interminable greetings.

You: 'How's the family?'

'Fine.'

'The wife?'

'Fine.'

65

'The children?'

'Fine.'

After a long pause, resume the salutations.

'How's work?'

'Fine.'

'Your friends, Ade and Jide?'

'They are well.'

'I thank God. So all is well then?'

Watch him as his ears suddenly prick up, as the Cameroonians say, 'like antelope way 'e hear news.'

'Well, as a matter of fact, not quite. You see, that's the reason I came to see you. I'm rather hard up for cash right now and . . .'

Like a flash you interrupt him.

'Wait here. I won't be a minute.'

You dash off to fetch Mr Atta your next door neighbour. Introduce him to your cousin.

'This is my brother Joseph. Do you remember what I told you two days ago?'

'About your cousin?' Thus Mr Atta, a bit bemused.

'That's right.' Thus you, looking desperate.

'Well I don't know if I should interfere in a family . . .'

'No, no, go ahead. Tell him.'

'Well, you said you were worried about some money you owed him.'

'What?' This from Cousin Joseph. He is so shocked he has half risen from the chair. 'What money? What debt? Who says I'm worried?'

Mr Atta attempts to press his story but Cousin Joseph will not let him.

'I came to see my cousin. Who's talking about money?' Thus Cousin Joseph.

As for you, sit back and relax. You are winning.

Perhaps I should explain what is happening. You see, Cousin Joseph is a Complete Nigerian. He knows he would never be forgiven if word got out that his blood relation had to go outside the family to borrow money in order to repay a debt to him. Your introduction of Mr Atta into the discussion was cooly calculated blackmail.

As Cousin Joseph makes a fast exist, you proudly say to Mr Atta: 'He's my favourite relation. We're very close!'

* * * * * * * * * *

NIGERIA is a class-ridden society. Do not be misled by the bluff, hearty fraternizations that rule any place where Nigerians are gathered in numbers. For underneath that veneer of unfettered companionability are rungs of structured snobberies.

Furthermore, be aware that Nigerian snootiness is money-based. Therefore, Nigerian uppishness stems from a mish-mash of levellers.

Our upper-classes are the middle-classes.

The ruling class does not rule.

The rich are public service bureaucrats, and the richest are government contract holders too poor to pay full income tax.

The working classes do not work, because they have the peasant classes, which abound with chiefs, to work for them.

It is true that Nigerians are mad about titles, but the successful Complete Nigerian is an aristocrat by inclination; he is inclined to say he is an aristocrat.

You can never accuse the successful Complete Nigerian of hiding his light under a bushel. He will proudly proclaim his title at the least opportunity. This is because he thinks he has earned it. If he was not born into it, he will buy it from a raffle of kingmakers; or, he will seek out a village head who is down on his luck, upon whom he will settle a princely sum in return for a meaningless title. If all else fails, he will claim it without compunction.

Ours must be the only country in the world where the initials J.P. represent a title other than Justice of the Peace: 'Jerusalem Pilgrim' — used by Christians. The custom arose out of jealousy for the Moslem Alhaji.

Ironically the Complete Nigerian is shy to declare himself a prince. He hates to be thought common.

Why is this so? The answer rests upon a mathematical rationale.

With the exception of a few states, where kingships and chieftancies automatically pass from father to eldest son, most Nigerian monarchies have more than one ruling house. These take turns to supply the reigning king. It is not uncommon to have as many as seven ruling houses around a throne, each with its own potential crown prince who is not necessarily the eldest male in the family.

The origins of this polyglot of royals is polygamy. In earlier times fertile harems ensured a multitudinous parade of princes who were dovetailed by a proliferation of princelings, who in turn were encouraged early in life to feed the prodigious production lines with offsprings, and thus kept the family numerically strong in the competition for the throne. Even today no Nigerian traditional ruler worthy of his majesty is a monogamist. His subjects would sneer at his stinginess.

Therefore, when a Nigerian tells you he is a

"Meet Alhaja, Chief, Doctor, Major General, Engr. . . . !"

prince, do not doubt him. It merely means he is one among a town-size population of princes.

No title, however, holds a greater aura for the Complete Nigerian than an honorary doctorate degree awarded by a roadside American university. Be careful when you address this man, for your entire relationship with him could stand or fall on whether or not you remember to call him 'doctor.' He may struggle to spell 'doctor' but it means music to his ears.

A recent addition to Nigerian etiquette is the requirement to address the Complete Nigerian by his full titles. This is especially evident in the newpapers.

Take a woman called Aina Too-Much.

No, let's not take her, let's visualize her.

She is married; she has made the holy pilgrimage to Mecca; she holds an honorary doctorate degree in science; she is an engineer by profession; she is a princess by birth, and a chief to boot; she retired from the Army Engineers with the rank of Major General, and has been elected to the Senate. She should be addressed as follows:

'Alhaja Senator Chief (Mrs) Princess (Dr) Major-General (rtd.) Engr. Aina Too-Much.

If she is a Complete Nigerian she will not resist you.

7

Soul Noise

WE Nigerians love noise. We invented it after all.

In the beginning God created His universe. He soon realized that the genesis of all subsequent existence was void and in pitch darkness. So, He put the sun, the moon and the stars in the blackness, to brighten things up a bit. Still He was not contented. He therefore created the dinosaurs and things like snakes, pigs, and wild beasts such as tigers and lions. But these were no good for company. And so God created man in His own image and likeness, hoping for a friend and looking forward to the occasional neighbourly chat over the garden fence.

The day God created the Nigerian was the most taxing of all. Even He, the Omnipotent, was exhausted, and we know for a fact that that day, the sixth day of a busy week, God put away His tools and rested.

Was this a mistake? It seems that if God had not taken a break that week-end, the history of the universe would have been different.

For while God rested, the Nigerian invented *Noise.*

The Bible story tells us that God was enjoying a shut-eye, when Adam and Eve stole away to eat an apple. God was so vexed He kicked them out of Paradise. Some apple!

Would you throw out your children and send them several million light years away from home just for picking a mango fruit off your tree? Let's face it, there had to be something more serious than a forbidden apple.

My story is that it was not even Adam and Eve who caused the expulsion from Paradise.

The Nigerian started it all. . .

It had been a peaceful Sunday afternoon and everywhere was serenity. A lazy breeze was blowing. As with all things in Heaven the temperature was perfect. Celestial voices sang dreamily melodious canticles to the accompaniment of angels strumming their harps.

It was against this background of a beautifully melancholic setting that *Noise* was heard for the first time in the Garden of Eden, breaking the peace of Paradise where until then all had been tranquil.

It was not your everyday noise, I hasten to point out, but a rumbustious, clamorous, disorderly, wilful type of noise guaranteed to crush the steadiest nerves.

Nigerian noise. Gargantuan noise, of a kind which only Nigerians can manufacture. Cantankerous, uneven, unexpected; loud and very annoying noise.

This was the *Noise* heard in Paradise that day.

Antelopes pricked up their ears and leapt up and down in fright. Elephants ran amok; and tigers trembled at the feet of the Maker. The cause of the unrest was soon identified.

'What is this strange sound?' the Lord God enquired from a somnolent angel reclining on a cloud nearby.

'Sire,' answered the rather dopey angel, 'it is the Nigerians. They are celebrating something they invented. They call it soul sound.'

The Almighty in his infinite mercy let the matter pass.

But the Nigerians grew bolder and wilder with their noises, raising hell in Paradise and adding new tricks to their repertoire of the noise pollution of the abode of God. At last the Great Forgiver had had enough.

75

'On a sabbath day?' thundered the Almighty, when one day the Nigerians again went wild with jubilation, praising the Lord in that peculiarly noisy way you will witness to this day in our revivalist get-togethers on beaches and outside the mosques frenzies, happy as larks and causing such a deafening uproar of religious enthusiasm God said to an angel, 'Where is Adam?'

Adam came into the Throne Room accompanied by Eve, his wife of many centuries. For ages she had henpecked him with the advice that he should speak up for himself and not kneel to every command from on high. Now she came with him to bone up his courage.

'Your Nigerian children,' the Lord God Almighty began, but the woman characteristically would not let Him finish.

'You gave us the Nigerians, Lord,' she said petulantly. 'Are they not your children also?'

The consternation on Adam's face spoke for all the congregations present at the interview. The Almighty was so displeased with Adam because he would not control the woman, He told them both to get out of His sight.

'And take your children with you!' added the Lord as he banished the lot of them to the Earth planet.

Because all the other expellees blamed the Nigerians for the loss to them of the peace and quiet of Paradise, they parted company with their erstwhile brethren, so that our ancestors became the Lost Tribe of Israel, on account of our noise-making.

As generations of Nigerians came and went, noise-making entered the very soul of our natural character; and today, no peoples on earth can compare with Nigerian noise.

The British fought gamely to suppress our noise-making when they ruled us. Their tyranny extended to crippling fines if you were heard shouting on court premises. You could not raise your own voice in a hospital when you visited the sick. You were discouraged from calling out to a friend across the aisle in church, although you had not seen him in a week.

But we fought back tenaciously. Our taxi drivers battled bravely honking needlessly; our music shop owners transferred their loud-speakers to the pavements; and how can we forget the soft-drinks vans criss-crossing our towns and cities blaring the most atrocious ditties advertising their fizzy brews?

We forced the British oppressors to retreat into ghettos. They thought they were snobs to live in what became known throughout Nigeria as GRA (Government Residential Area). These were salubrious, well laid out and exclusive enclaves from which Nigerians were generally excluded. But it was the British segregationists who suffered.

The loneliness of their exclusion from Nigerian noise drove many into madness.

What else would you call it when couples swopped wives, when housewives took domestic servants as lovers, and the community generally ruined its liver drinking itself to death? All this happened to the British colonial masters. And all because they sought escape from Nigerian noise.

A successful European buys a house in the country and spends the best years of his life seeking solitude. He climbs mountains and joins a country club where he goes to smoke cigars and read boring newspapers just to get away from his family. So stringent are the customs in some of their establishments a club member may not speak to another unless he has noticed that the brooding fellow is on fire and appears unaware of it.

In Nigeria you are regarded with suspicion if you seek solitude, climb mountains and have a house in the country. Our clubs are places of merriment where members arrive to jabber, to chatter and to exchange confidences in whispers so loud their voices can be heard all the way home.

78

When the peace of your home is invaded by street players on a quiet Sunday morning you may not go out and tell them to beat it. The Complete Nigerian must go out with a long-suffering half smile to reward the unsolicited noisy jollity before returning to bawl at his family and demand to know who the fool was who left the gates open to admit the bastards.

When two long-lost English friends meet, they find it sufficient to stammer out their emotions:

'I say John Bull, is it not?' says one.

'Well, I never. . .!' says the other.

Anything further is considered exhibitionist and in bad taste.

In Nigeria we make a noise. I mean to say, we make one hell of a noise! For the joy of meeting again must be heard as well as seen.

The English dictionary describes the word 'salute' as, 'To greet with words or with a gesture or with a kiss; to greet; to hail; to honour formally by a discharge of cannon. . .'

Among us Nigerians a reunion is a salutation. By which I do not mean greeting, 'with a gesture or with a kiss. . .' I mean honouring informally with a discharge of verbal cannon.

Summon the neighbours to witness. They in turn will hoot and shout. Women will ululate;

and if it does not take the strong intervention of neighbours to separate you from your friend, you have not had a good reunion, I tell you!

Astonishingly, there are places where it is not fashionable to make a noise. But you must think very hard and decide this for yourself, for no-one can help you.

8

The Chairman

OF all the beguiling roles the Complete Nigerian is called upon to perform in his community, none so easily inflates his ego as the invitation to be chairman at a social event. It is his chance to play God.

No social gathering is complete without a chairman. Such is the passion for a presider that a pack of young Nigerian tearaways would elect a chairman to guide them through their first dirty week-end.

A chairman is appointed to direct a public lecture, a wedding reception, a christening party, a wake-keeping, a political rally, or a football match. Even though the doddering fellow may be too infirm to take the ceremonial 'first kick,' his presence will lend excitement and attract hundreds of spectators who might otherwise have stayed home.

Ours is a patriarchal society with a craving for father figures. Hence, a popular chairman is a dictator, a bully and a know-all who is not averse to self-promotion.

A chairman is chosen firstly, for his upright social standing; and then, for his money. The two qualities are considered synonymous in Nigeria, so that a person without money is not considered socially vertical. The chairman is expected to make a large donation, in return for the privilege of the spotlight that will shine on him throughout the proceedings.

On the other hand, the status of a chairman is thought to reflect the quality of a social event. It is therefore not unusual that a well-known public figure who has been advertised as chairman of a forthcoming rave-up learns of his commitment only when he sees his own face smiling at him from posters plastered all over town.

Since he was not asked, and since the organisers did not expect him to turn up, a suitable excuse for his absence will be tendered at the shindig, and it will tickle him mercilessly to read in the newspapers that the burden of paying for the privilege passed to a social rival who was so flattered he gave a donation quite out of this world.

There are times when money does not influence the choice of a chairman, however.

Sometimes the chairman is a high-profile intellectual, or a professional dissident seeking martyrdom through turgid newspaper essays which are outstanding for their anarchic social commentaries and ramshackle literary flow.

This type of chairman is more frequently found in the company of merry-makers swilling Coca-Cola with champagne motions.

Anybody with a bit of money or the right intellectual arrogance can serve as a chairman, but it takes more than material possession and academic brain power to be a successful Complete Nigerian Chairman.

Here are a few tips on how to achieve that distinction:

- If you are the moneyed type, admit that you have not been asked because you can deliver the square root of 27. Do not bother therefore to prepare a written speech. Speaking *ex tempore* will mean your address is long and rambling, which is a standard requirement of a successful Complete Nigerian Chairman. Besides, you will be praised for what you wore on the occasion not for what you said.

- For your attire, lace fabric is always a winner. People should know the colour of your underwear.

- Hang a giant gold chain on your neck.
- Wear a cheap digital wrist-watch dipped in gold.
- Wear an 18-carat gold name-bracelet.
- Wear fancy buttons.
- Wear multi-tone court slippers in violently clashing colours.
- Arrive late. A chairman who arrives disgustingly late is sure to be popularly greeted with glorious cheers of relief.
- When called upon to speak by the master of ceremony begin with a time-worn joke which everybody knows by heart. Your audience will fall apart laughing:

'Ladies and gentlemen, I am retired but not tired! When I was appointed to be the chairman of this occasion, I asked who else would be coming. I was told that Pa Oluwole, Daddy Joseph and Adio-goldsmith would be here. I couldn't believe that I should be given the honour of chairman when there were such distinguished elders available. After all, what have I achieved in life?'

This is a sly attack on your social rivals, a ploy which is held in high esteem by Nigerian audiences who love to decipher the coded assaults.

Fierce whispers of, 'The chair! Let's hear the chairman!' will rent the air as ushers and self-appointed stewards rise to hush-up the interruptions.

As the pandemonium grows into wolf-whistles, cheers, inexplicable laughter and more shouts of 'Please, let's hear the chairman,' you stand your ground smiling benignly. Do not interfere in the bedlam. We Nigerians easily become restive when listening to a speech, and we are prone to relieve our restlessness with undisciplined interjections. Everyone is having a good time and your chairmaship is a success.

*   *   *   *   *   *   *   *   *   *

● If you are the intellectual type remember that the organizers who asked you to be chairman did not expect to hear money jingling in your pockets. They would much rather smell you. Dress accordingly.

● A pair of unwashed jeans trousers and a rough tie-dye shirt of uncertain maturity always helps.

● What you lack by way of the readies you must make up for in erudition.

● All successful intellectual chairman have a sense of showmanship. Therefore, practice your written speech before the bathroom mirror and learn to emphasise catchphrases with appropriate grimaces.

● Your big ally on the night is the master of ceremony. It would be worth your while to form his acquaintance before hand. Get him to introduce you as a 'man who has done a lot for our community in particular, and Nigeria in general.' This phrase always has Nigerians stamping their feet and clapping their hands wildly.

● If you studied abroad the m.c. must be induced to make frequent references to 'the time when our distinguished chairman was overseas struggling to bring home the golden fleece.'

And when you are called upon to speak, remember to enunciate your words through clenched teeth. People will form a most excellent impression if you sound like an English upperclass twit speaking a Nigerian vernacular.

Fill your monologue with a healthy mix of long English texts and snappy Nigerian vernacular. This shows you are so highly educated you have lost your knowledge of Nigerian vernacular. Yet by interjecting your speech with an occasional vernacular, it shows you are making a brave effort to identify with the common people:

'My dear friends, *biko*, if I gravitate towards bombination, do not, *ejo*, scruple to expostulate your disapprobation. Notwithstanding, authorise me to asserverate that the agenda of our national politico-economic orientation must be masterminded by the *talakawa*. As our *diokpas* used to say, *'Salaam-ailekum.'*

Your bewildered audience will disperse praising your scholarship. Or, to put it another way, your mystified assemblage will demobilize to panegyrize the evanescence of your expository political ethos so fugaciously verbalized.

9

The Village Orators

THE Complete Nigerian orator who has been to school, who has read Shakespeare, and who can recite the whole of Mark Antony's funeral oration for the late Julius Caesar, has only silver on his tongue. Forget him.

The man you want to hear is the Complete Nigerian Orator who has never lived in an urban environment: the village orator.

He is a master craftsman of the double entendre which he conceals in a flurry of proverbs.

He is wickedest when you least expect it. Such as for example, at a mediation.

His display of ornamental speech begins with the prayers preceding the ceremonial splitting of kolanuts. The man who has the honour of performing this ritual is Egbuna Kedu, an old boy with three missing front teeth and some evidence of past hair on his scrawny head. He speaks:

'Fellow elders, you mothers, my sons and daughters, may the spirits of our ancestors, may Ogidigidi the Great himself, bless us all. *(Shouts of 'amen' all round.)* May the enemy of our enemies triumph over his adversaries, but may he not celebrate his victory with our wives! Is it not so? *(Shouts of 'yes, yes, it is so!')* And the reason we are gathered here this evening, may it be resolved. Everyone to whom I am going to distribute a piece of kolanut knows the admonition of the tom-tom droms; 'Do not eat my food if you bear me a grudge; do not bear me a grudge after you've eaten my food.'

'Why are we here? They say it is he whose moustache is on fire who smells the burning. Who else can settle our quarrels but ourselves? It is the mother whose son has been eaten by a witch who best knows the evils of witchcraft.

How can a man for whom a fire has been lit by his enemies rub oil on himself and lie close to the fire? That is what I want to know from these children who are quarrelling among themselves. Ignorance is the privilege of youth; alertness is the virtue of the old. Proverb has it that it is the man whose barn is full of yams who must watch out for thieves. You (he turns fiercely to his nephew, Mba, whose disagreement with his wife Abigail is the cause of the arbitration) how long have I been telling you that one of these days your temper will get you into trouble?'

Mba rises in anger: 'Uncle, you haven't heard me yet but you are judging me already?' .

'Shut up! Shut your mouth!' Egbuna Kedu shouts at him. 'So now you will tell me how to speak in public? Look at him! The butterfly thinks it is a bird!'

Actually Mba is safe from his uncle's wrath. He knows his uncle's private views about Abigail who has not conceived a child after five years of marriage. Abigail blames Mba's many affairs with other women, but Mba believes that Abigail is physiologically barren and would divorce her if he could. Abigail's family are old allies, however, and Mba does not have the full support of his own family.

Abigail's mother on the other hand backs her daughter to the hilt. When earlier she tried to arrest the growing estrangement, before it became known to the rest of the family, she told her son-in-law bluntly that he must stop running around.

'A man who wants to make foam must piss on the same spot,' she counselled him; adding, 'A goat that is owned by several people will die of hunger.'

Oshinuka, the local barber, takes the floor.

He is Mba's cousin twice removed but they grew up together like brothers. He too thinks the union with Abigail should be dissolved.

'My elders, my mothers, my brothers and sisters,' he begins. 'God bless us all. May our fathers live long, and may we younger ones live to be old men like them. I cannot say too much because I am in the presence of older people, and even if I do not agree with the way my "father" Egbuna, whose life has been an inspiration to us all . . . even if I do not agree with the way he has just silenced my "brother" Mba, proverb says you don't tell an old man his mouth is smelling. That is all I have to say.'

He sits down to murmurs of approval for a clever intervention. He has dared to tell Egbuna Kedu his rough dismissal of Mba's protest is wrong.

But the old man hits back immediately: 'Our forefathers had the saying that the elders of a community are the voice of God. *(Pause)*. Any man or woman present here who does not seek old age should put his hand up. *(There are no takers.)* God bless us all. . . God give you young ones children — good children who will know not to interrupt you in public. . .'

There is a dramatic pause amid shouts of 'amen!' and then: 'Oshinuka, I pray for you that you reach my age . . .' *This is recognized as a veiled threat of a curse and sure enough there are pleas from the congregation: 'Papa forgive him; he did not mean to be rude; it is his youth.'*

Egbuna Kedu presses his advantage.

'Mba is my son,' he resumes, directing a harsh glare at Oshinuka. 'I can say whatever I like to him in public and even you, Mr Know-all, I can tell you off any day, any time. Don't think because you are taller than me I cannot discipline you. A short man is not a small boy.'

The unexpected tension within Mba's family group affords the leader of Abigail's delegation the opportunity to put on a virtuoso performance. Erasmus Eeteh wades in to exploit what he sees as a disagreement between Egbuna Kedu and Oshinuka, but his strategy is couched in a series of proverbs.

'My brothers,' he begins smoothly, 'Trouble does not blow a whistle to announce its approach.

'Our people say that no matter how deep down you dive into water to eat a banana, the skin will rise to the surface. After all what is a secret? Is there a greater secret than that between a man and his wife, but does the whole world not know what took place between them nine months later?

93

'We are here because our son Mba and our daughter Abigail are quarrelling . . . quarrelling, I tell you. With whose permission? That is what I want to know. I say this openly to Abigail. If your father was alive today the ground would be taller than you!'

Abigail looks down at her feet. It does not disturb her that her uncle should round on her in public. He is employing a strategy of Nigerian mediation.

The rules are that a mediator should begin by blasting his own side in explicit language. This suggests he is open-minded and prepared to find a compromise. But this is a trick to disguise his attack on the other party for whom he reserves his most trenchant proverbs.

Erasmus thinks Mba is a rat. It is a view he has expressed in the privacy of his own family compound. But at the mediation he disguises his private views in proverbs and parables.

He says to Mba, 'My son, do you remember the day you came to fetch your wife Abigail from my home? You were so eager for her. I said to you, Wait a while. The horse must eat while the grass is growing. So you gave me another fifty naira. There will be children. Be patient, my son. My late uncle, whose spirit is watching us now, just as the spirits of our ancestors are with us here . . . God bless us all . . . May water never cease to rise in our wells. . . God bless you mothers who have given your husbands strong, healthy sons. . .My uncle was in great form that night; and then he suddenly took off to join his ancestors! *(Ther are murmurs of lament all around and much shaking of heads in sorrow).* And you my brother Egbuna, do you remember the night you came to pay Abigail's bride price? I watched you dance. I thought to myself, look at this old dog dancing like a man whose pubic hairs have not turned grey. No wonder you still fathered a son eight years ago. Won't you ever grow old?'

Egbuna laughs mirthfully, slaps a thigh and retorts, 'That was what I told Mama Ibisu the other night. She was looking at me in that way. I told her, don't look at me like that, won't you ever grow old?'

Everyone bursts into laughter. Mama Ibisu, the mother of Ayeni, Egbuna's youngest son protests good humouredly.

'He talks as though it is not I who needs the sleep,' she says in a low whisper which is heard by many. 'That man has the loins of a tiger.'

'Stop bragging,' Mama Tinu admonishes her before taking the floor herself.

Mama Tinu has graduated into the men's

world through advanced age. She is female to be sure but to the ancient men around her she is no longer sexually appetizing and she might just as well be a man.

'Welcome to our home,' she begins, but she is immediately halted by Abigail's mother.

'Auntie, do you not mean, welcome to *our* home?'

Abigail's mother did not miss a thing. The inflexion in Mama Tinu's voice validated her intervention.

'It is so, my daughter. It is so. Welcome to *your* home. Abigail is my daughter, she is my wife. May God bless us all. May menopause not arrive too soon for Abigail. She is young. She is strong. I keep asking myself, why does she not bear child? What curse is this?'

'There is no curse!' Abigail's mother leaps in to defend her daughter.

'Well, what is it then? Why does she not conceive?' Mama Tinu answers back. 'My grandson is strong.'

A quarrel breaks out between the two women. This is signalled by the flow of proverbs tumbling fast and furious.

'Your grandson is strong? Bah! Khaki is not leather; appearances do not count,' Abigail's mother sneers.

'What do you mean?' Mama Tinu shouts back. 'If you are pointing an accusing finger at a person, remember that at the same time four of your own fingers are pointing accusingly at you in reverse.'

Abigail's mother is a fighter, however, and is not about to have her daughter's reputation sullied.

'Life is unfair,' she says stoutly. 'It is the arse which farts but it is the head that gets a knock in rebuke. Mba has many women. Why has he not had a child by another woman? He is a man, yes; all lizards bask in the sun in the same fashion, but can you tell if one of them has stomach ache?'

With that last remark, Mama Tinu can no longer contain herself. She is visibly seething with rage. 'A person who has relatives in the market place should not throw stones into the market. You cannot make insinuations and expect to get away with them. A man who is sought out by women has something going for him'.

There is a sardonic smile on her face but Abigail's mother is equal to it.

'I respect you Mama Tinu. You are our mother. But the sun does not shine from Mba's backside. If he is upset by my remarks it is

97

because he who shits on the road will find flies on her way back.'

'It is enough!' barks Egbuna Kedu at last. 'When women talk there is an end to reasoning. I say to you both, he who casts ashes into the wind will be covered in ashes. We came to settle a quarrel between our son and our daughter. Do not divert us from our purpose.

'When there's confusion in a market place you don't have to tell even a mad man that people are running for safety. Let us parents and elders be neutral in this matter. Proverb says that an elder who is kind to youth will never starve.'

'Yes,' Erasmus adds sagely, 'the child who says his mother shall not sleep shall itself not sleep. One man alone cannot battle with a multitude.'

'Precisely,' enjoins Egbuna Kedu. 'When the elephant falls dead who will bear its corpse away? Does the crocodile shed tears of sorrow?'

'No, and you don't have to tell a deaf man that war has broken out.' This from Erasmus.

'Thank you my brother,' rejoins Egbuna Kedu. 'Our fore-fathers had the saying that all dogs eat rubbish but it is the unlucky ones that get caught. Shall we say we are unlucky? All families have their problems, but should everybody in this village know about our problems? Proverb says that a man who is wearing borrowed clothes should not be seen dancing at the head of a procession. But look at families less known than ours. They dare to show off when we are around, as though they wore any clothers before the white man came! I am saddened that the best of our young people go to places like Lagos and even as far away as Kano. What are they looking for in those places? A man should remain in his ancestral environment. Look at the monkey. It is spectacular as it leaps from tree to tree. That is because the forest is populated with trees. Otherwise, can the monkey show off in a desert? So you see there is no place like home!' (This is greeted by a round of applause.)

'I speak for Abigail's mother and all the family,' Erasmus says gently. 'We want peace between our two children. We want the past forgotten and a new start made. A man said to his enemy, "When you bit me in the arse you did not look to check the state of my bottom. When I bite you in the nose therefore, why should I look at the mucus in your nostrils?"

'Mba, Abigail, I say this to both of you. When next a heated argument develops between you two, let one give way to the other. The Hausa people have a saying, *Shuru-shuru bat-soro ba*. (Because I am quiet it doesn't mean

I am a coward.) A vulture has no need for a barber. This is another saying of the Hausa people. Learn that wisdom. Only a people who have no one to guide them fail to receive guidance. God bless us all. *(Eager cries of 'amen!')* I want you to know today that a man who acknowledges his madness is on the way to being healed. So I tell you both, Mba, Abigail, finish this madness between you two. Go home and take your clothes off, lock your door firmly to all callers. We won't mind. (Laughter). God will take care of the rest.' (More laughter).

Mba and Abigail knew all along that divorce was not on the cards. The object of the mediation was really to pronounce that verdict publicly.

The time to close the session arrives and it is Erasmus who fills it with a parting piece of superb oratory:

'When the monkey was asked how he got his fleas, he pointed at the other monkey,' he says his voice quivering with emotion. 'What would anyone benefit from apportioning blame? Remember the story of the tortoise? One morning his neighbours found him trussed up and gagged. He was covered in filth and rubbish. His father-in-law had done it to him, to humiliate him publicly, for beating his wife. "Serves him right," passersby said. By nightfall, however, when the neighbours found him still trussed up and gagged and covered in filth and rubbish by the roadside they said, "What kind of a father-in-law is this who humiliates his daughter's husband before the whole world?" It is not enough that you believe yourself to be right, my children; you must not seek redress beyond reason. . . God bless us all. . . *(Amen!)* Mba, may God stoke your fire so that soon enough Abigail's fertility will thrill with the cry of a grandson for me. *(There's much twittering and meaningful winks among the mediators).* Did you hear me, Mba? A son, that is what I must have. Don't let Abigail defeat you by having a girl. Show her you are the man. Or, don't you have the strength? Abigail, tell us, has he no power. . .?'

Amid more voluntary prayers all around the session breaks up.

Everyone goes home doubled up with laughter.

10

The Nigerian Factor

THE Complete Nigerian is a born philosopher. Not many people know this.

Behind that exterior of a jocular, seemingly frivolous disposition is a profound mind girdled by a set of philosophical principles collectively known as *The Nigerian Factor.*

Never underestimate *The Nigerian Factor.* It is the basic truth by which the Complete Nigerian dominates his environment.

For instance, it instructs his business acumen.

I once stood in a queue on Lekki Beach in Lagos, waiting my turn at the *suya* barbecue.

'Twenty-five naira,' said the cook.

I paid up.

Immediately behind my son and me was a man looking the worse for wear. He had placed the same order as us.

'Twenty naira,' I heard the cook say to him.

I went back to the cook. 'Mallam why did you charge me five naira more?'

I knew the answer without being told. I must have seemed to him a man who could afford five naira more than the fellow behind me. However, what the cook said was a barefaced lie.

'I forgot,' said the idiot without looking away from the charcoal fire.

He should have said to me, *'Oga,* I think say you get money pass the other *massa.'* And he would have confessed to being influenced by *The Nigerian Factor.*

If you are Chief Olu Hassan-Obi, an Ordinary Nigerian tendering for a contract, and you concern yourself with the financial and technical requirements of the contract as published in the newspaper announcement; if you call in your technical advisers, your accountants, your lawyers, and if these highly qualified experts put together the detailed facts and figures that would enable you formulate a genuine tender and reach a sound business decision — if you are this type of a procedural businessman, my advice to you is that you drop out of sight, return to your village and resume the manual profession of palm wine tapper which gave you your success in the first place. For you have no aptitude for big business in Nigeria.

While you were busying yourself chasing

103

technical specialists and organizing skilful lawyers, the Complete Nigerian, your rival, was deep in philosophy, trying to discover *The Nigerian Factor* in the contract. Unlike you, he knows that *The Nigerian Factor* will direct the outcome of the contract tender.

For instance, who are the members of the contracts award committee? How can they be reached? How can they be influenced? Who are the friends fronting for them in their secret businesses? Who are their relatives? Is there a political authority to overrule the committee? Who are the wives the committee members sleep with when they give their mistresses a rest? Are they important? *Everyman has his price.* Who is that everyman on the committee? What is his price? Who stands to benefit from the scheme in order that Joe Public may have it at all? These questions are determinant of *The Nigerian Factor.*

On the appointed day, all the competing tenders are ceremonially opened in the presence of assembled Press photographers. But behind the scenes and in conformity with *The Nigerian Factor*, the Complete Nigerian knows he has won the contract long before that public display of impartiality.

After you have lost, your rival will rub your

nose in it by going straight out to purchase a new car.

You will learn also that he has not only added a new wife to his coterie of supporters, but that to appease an earlier wife whom he married in a small and undistinguished religious ceremony twenty years previously, he has bought a massive collection of gold jewellery. On their first outing together he will fit out himself in the same dress material as his wives to emphasize the domestic harmony.

All this is exhausting. So, afterwards, the Complete Nigerian who is now an even more successful business entrepreneur, will take himself off on an expensive vacation in Europe.

Upon his return from holiday and fully rested, the Complete Nigerian will ask himself a philosophical question: Does a person necessarily have to complete a contract simply because he has received a huge mobilization fee?

The Nigerian Factor says he does not.

Machines

THE Complete Nigerian is easily held in thrall by machines. Be careful therefore.

Before you put him in charge of delicate scientific machinery or combustible equipment, bear in mind that his heart may be in the right place but that his respect for engineering apparati is conditioned by *The Nigerian Factor*.

You say to the Complete Nigerian, 'Your job is to keep an eye on this dial. If the needle falls below the figure "8" it means the machine is not performing properly. If, on the other hand, the needle should rise above the number "15", it would also mean that there is something wrong. In either circumstance you must turn off the equipment forthwith and summon me to the emergency.'

At first your conscientious Complete Nigerian will attend to your instructions with a devotion approaching fanaticism.

Every hour of every working day during the next fortnight, he will sit diligently before the apparatus, his vigilance glued resolutely to the appliance. Then, soon enough, he will fall in love with the machine.

· He will grow to question your lack of faith in such a reliable machine. That needle you asked him to watch on the dial has never dropped below '8' nor has it risen above '15'. Whatever made you think it might?

'*Oga*, the machine good. It is Japanese,' he will tell you, complimenting you for making the choice. 'The machine work fine like strong German medicine,' he will exclaim.

Three weeks after his little speech, however, a tremendous bang will signal to you that the roof of your factory has gone up in flames. Such is the power of *The Nigerian Factor*

For, three days earlier, while at work, your Complete Nigerian operator exercised his liberty, a fundamental cornerstone of *The Nigerian Factor*, by failing to pay further attention to the dial.

It was a nice day and he was feeling good and fancy-free. He decided to pay a visit to the machine room next door, where he swapped jokes with colleagues. He reasoned that for more than two weeks he had faithfully observed the readings on the dial and nothing untoward had occurred to justify his continued undivided attention. So, he went on a little excursion. No damage was done by his absence.

Two days later, with the sun once again bathing down upon the environment and, filled again with that feeling of well-being, with nothing better to do than watch that dial — a dial remember, that had not failed in three weeks — he strolled away from the premises to take in the breeze and relieve the drudgery.

Your machine chose that moment to blow up.

'No condition is permanent,' your operator

will say to himself, rejecting any blame and invoking a lesser known tenet of *The Nigerian Factor*. But to you he will say, '*Oga*, you were right, Japanese machines have to be watched day and night . . . Chief, I think next time we should buy German. Their machines are strong and you don't have to watch them all the time!'

If you are inclined at this point to murder him, to shut him up, remember that his successor may be another Complete Nigerian, and that most Nigerian technicians at one time or another in their careers are prone to *The Nigerian Factor*.

* * * * * * * * *

Suggested motto on a coat-of-arms for the Union of Complete Nigerian Technicians: 'Give us the job and we shall finish the tools.'

The Market-place

ON a clear day you can hear forever in the Nigerian market-place; seller and buyer are haggling at the top of their voices as each party manoeuvres to secure a price advantage over the other.

The Complete Nigerian buyer as well as seller, has no faith in fixed prices.

The retailer believes his price is fair only if he has hurt the pocket of the buyer, while the buyer seeks to tire out the seller with haggling, and come off with a bargain.

Therefore, although in most parts of the world a tag tells you the exact price of a product for sale, we prefer the friendly vexation of price wangling in our markets. So, we have a custom we call 'bargain', which means haggle, and which can be a hassle.

It begins when the seller confidently demands an extravagant forty-five naira for a product she knows is worth twenty naira. In reply, the buyer, having done a quick mental arithmetic, offers a price he hopes is well below the market value. Then the two go into a friendly squabble.

The buyer is at a disadvantage because he does not know what figure the seller will eventually settle for. If he makes the mistake of offering a 'fair' price i.e., a price high enough to fetch the seller a handsome profit, the retailer will utter a feeble protest before accepting to settle. When this happens it is too late for the buyer to go down in price. Therefore, the trick is to make as low an offer as you dare and observe the speed with which the seller rejects it.

If he says 'no' with a slow shake of the head, the buyer knows he is close to the mark. But it also means he has not challenged the seller sufficiently to force a protracted negotiation, which is the proper way to ensure a fair price.

If the buyer's first offer is turned down flat with a vehemence verging on rudeness, he must stand his ground; for it is a sign that the seller realizes he has started off lower than the buyer would have tolerated.

If, however, the seller makes a plea for understanding with words such as, 'Ah, customer, you know yourself how the market is hard these days. . .,' the buyer must watch his step. He is about to be eaten raw.

'Bargain' is a commonplace exercise in the Nigerian market-place. By itself it is an ordinary substance of *The Nigerian Factor*. But the intervention of foreigners brings out the worst kind of *The Nigerian Factor* in the market-place.

Not so long ago, I had the occasion to conduct a small group of visiting Black American dentists and medical doctors on a tour of the Lagos area.

They had heard about the 'interesting' Nigerian convention of haggling in the market-place and were keen to try themselves out. The poor innocents thought it would be a walk-over sparring with Nigerian market *mammies*. They thought it was a game for amateurs.

I did my best to school them in the art. But foreigners will be foreigners. They wanted to enjoy themselves. By all means, I said to them, have fun, but there are ground rules.

'The first requirement is to arrange your face,' I said clearly enough.

The face is where the market *mammy* searches before she declares her price. Are your intentions serious, or are you merely browsing? If it is the latter be sure she is self-trained to read it in your face. She would then name a price so unbelievably high you should know she has deliberately insulted your intelligence. She is telling you to go away.

A second pre-higgle preparation is your overall appearance. It is no good asking the Nigerian market *mammy* the price of an article if she thinks you do not look as though you can afford it. So, if you have a million naira to spend she wants you to look a million dollars. With that she would be pleased to let you argue her price all day long, even to the extent of you pretending to lose your temper.

In the end you will come away with the satisfaction of not knowing whether or not you've been flayed!

111

I told my American visitors all this.

I explained that they were on their own. I could only act as their guide, because any intervention from me would provoke a stream of abuse. As a local boy it was assumed that I knew the score and I would be denounced as playing for the opposition if I was seen to be coaching them. I therefore suggested the selection of a spokesperson from their ranks.

The choice of Alvin for that role was my first mistake. I had selected him because he had good teeth. I didn't know that a fine dentist could make such a poor actor.

The second mistake was to tell my friends to reorganize themselves sartorially and to remember to construct their countenances in such a manner they would not be thought ignorant foreigners.

The Brothers went wild with the preparations.

When I arrived the following morning I swear I walked straight through them. I could not recognize any of my friends among the ragamuffins waiting in the hotel lobby. Even to this day, I refuse to believe they hoped to pass themselves off as Nigerians by their motley attires.

Two or three of them were actually draped in curtains purloined from their hotel rooms. They said they were Benin chiefs. The rest were just plain silly.

I had to send the lot of them back to their rooms to change, and that set us off in a bad temper.

My third mistake was to think that all dentists have a head for figures.

I said to my man Alvin: 'What you do is quite simple. When the market *mammy* pronounces her price you must divide that figure into two equal halves. Then you multiply one half by three. Next, you deduct her original offer from the result of your multiplication. Now take the figure of the original offer once more and divide it into four parts. Add the quarter to the result of your earlier multiplication. The figure you obtain is the fair price and this is the only way haggling with the Nigerian market *mammy* makes any sense.'

'Gotcha!' said Alvin flamboyantly and we were on our way.

We duly arrived at Jankara Market, in the heart of Lagos Island. It used to be said that you could buy anything at Jankara Market — anything from freshly dug up human skulls to apparels stolen from your clothes line the night before.

Alvin ignored all these dangers and made straight for a stall filled to half its capacity by the giant figure of a maiden on whose breasts a toddler was learning mountaineering.

113

'How much?' said Alvin abruptly, handling a trinket with such cold disdain I really thought he was about to hurl the thing at the woman in disgust. I had warned him to be circumspect and this was his way of carrying out my orders.

The giantess dropped the baby carelessly and rose to her full height of twenty feet which was most disconcerting for me at 6ft 1 inch. It also had the effect of shutting out the daylight in the stall.

She gave Alvin her price. Actually she did not simply give it. She declaimed it to the hearing of half the market. I was all for paying up and making a fast get-away, but I heard Alvin say fearlessly, 'Nonsense, woman. I wouldn't give you a dime more than. . .'

I could see he was stuck for a figure. He could not reason the mathematical route I'd taught him fast enough.

'Damn!' he growled, 'This ain't worth a dime any how.' He threw the trinket back into a tray. 'Say, lady, how much you wanna tell me this thing is really worth, seeing as I've made my gambit? C'mon, c'mon, its your go. Say something!'

Of course there was no answer to this from the woman. She didn't know what the hell he was talking about.

'Pete, how am I doing?' Alvin called out to me.

'Dandy, just dandy.' What else could I say?

Encouraged by my response, our spokesman summoned the gang to follow him out. I had told him he could pretend to walk away should the negotiations come to a standstill. I had assured him that if he played it right he should expect to be called back.

But I had not counted on Alvin's extravagant campaign tactics. He went heavily over the top in the dramatic role he had fashioned for himself. I hadn't asked him to be aggressive and utterly impossible.

'Let's get outta here,' he commanded the others, 'This lady ain't in business.'

His exit was grossly premature. Besides, the giantess had not attended my briefing session and was therefore not privy to the fact that Alvin was required to play games. All she knew was that she was not going to take nonsense from a jumped-up twerp. And a foreigner at that. The woman was born with *The Nigerian Factor* in her bones.

She addressed herself to me:

'You brought a mad man to my stall,' she cursed in the vernacular. 'It is early in the day. Do I know you? Have I ever crossed your path?

116

Why do you wish to bring me misfortune by bringing a bad customer to my stall so early in the day? Have my enemies sent you to provoke me?'

The accusations poured out in a torrent as *The Nigerian Factor* fired up her blood in a boiling rage.

Alvin meanwhile had assembled the others outside the stall waiting expectantly to be summoned by a chastized market *mammy* ready to play the game.

'Get yourself and your evil friends away from my stall,' the gargantuan mistress thundered at me. She summoned her next door neighbour to witness: 'Have you seen this kind of thing before? So early in the day, this man brings some foreign lunatics to my stall. Maybe it is better for me to shut down for the day. This is bad luck. What have I done to deserve this?' She went on and on.

Suddenly jumbo-sized market *mammies* built like *sumo* wrestlers began to roll out of their stalls. Everyone had a nasty word for me.

'She's not going to call us back, is she?' Alvin asked forlornly as I placed myself securely in the protective custody of the group.

'You blew it!' I said crossly.

'Why? I walked away — slowly away, I may add. I did as you asked.'

'She recognized you as a foreigner,' I added rather unkindly.

'What's that got to do with anything?' Alvin was upset.

'It's *The Nigerian Factor*,' I told him.

'What's that mean?'

'I can't explain it.'

'But Nigerians love foreigners,' Alvin said defensively. 'Everyone's been good to us. People at the hotel, the staff, they all want to know about the States? Total strangers have bought us drinks, asked to have our addresses and promised to write.'

'Yes, Nigerians are good to foreigners,' I agreed, 'until *The Nigerian Factor* rears its head.'

The Bureaucrat

THERE was a time when Nigerian bureaucracies, were staffed by people who answered only to initials.

Bureaucrats were so incognito even their intimate friends dared not address them by their real names.

'Is the E.O. in?'

'No, sir, he's gone to see the D.E. about the S.I.'s C.V.*

No policeman with any self-respect answered to 'officer;' he thrust his chest out to 'p.c.'* which became 'o.c.,'* from the day he was promoted lance-corporal and permitted to wear a V-shaped stripe on the sleeve of his tunic.

'You see that man?' a father would whisper to his son as an important civil servant rode past proudly on his new bicycle, 'He is the c.c. to the A.D.O.-2 who plays tennis with the D.O. and the S.P. when the S.R. is visiting from h.q.'*

Civil servants were so bureaucratized they even had their own Bible and Koran. The formidable, habit-forming tome was called 'General Orders.' It regulated the personal and public lives of the civil servant. It told him how to behave, how not to behave; how to be himself, how not to be himself.

The G.O. was held in such blind regard that

E.O.	— Education Officer	S.I.	— Sanitation Inspector
D.E.	— District Engineer	C.V.	Curricula vitae
c.c.	— chief clerk	A.D.O	— Assistant District Officer
D.O.	— District Officer	(cadet)	
S.R.	— Senior Resident.	S.P.	— Superintendent of Police
o.c.	— Officer in charge	p.c.	— police constable

when a friend of mine sought to write an expose titled, 'What I know about the G.O.', he took the precaution to hand in notice of his early retirement before he ventured to inform his superiors of his plans.

As an experienced civil servant, he submitted the internal memo to his Higher Executive Officer, who forwarded it to the Assistant Secretary for onward transmission to the Permanent Secretary, through the Senior Assistant Secretary, who sought the advice of the Deputy Permanent Secretary.

Despite all this, he was told his application could not be entertained as he was still a servant of the Crown. Then he was issued with a query (in triplicates) ordering him to explain why he should not be disciplined for making threats against Her Majesty's loyal administration.

In those grim days of British-style bureaucracy injunctions stamped on files meant what they said:

URGENT — needing prompt action;

CONFIDENTIAL — a secret with a small 's'

SECRET — confidential with a big 'C'

TOP SECRET — a secret with a big 'S'

When a file was marked 'b.u. on April 1' it was not an April fool caper. It was 'brought up' on April 1.

Mercifully the departure of the British autocrats permitted the ascendance of the *The Nigerian Factor* in our bureaucracy; and with it came the Complete Nigerian bureaucrat.

The Complete Nigerian civil servant unlike his predecessor is not self-effacing behind an array of coded titles. You meet him here, you see him there, and you talk to him yonder. He is eager to make your acquaintance. He takes you into little corners to confide in you.

For instance, he tells you how much it would cost you to have your file speeded up, which I think is very nice.

He is also quick to trust you. Although you hardly know each other, he will take down your name and home address and visit you, to meet your family and to chat about his financial problems. He expects you to help him solve his financial problems because you want your file to move faster. After all, what are friends for?

Under the revolution of *The Nigerian Factor*, official secrets are no longer official. They are known to messengers who learn them from filing clerks, who have discussed them at length with stenographers, who are frequently surprised by how much the bosses tell their receptionists about the other woman, who is the wife.

Military rule took us a step further. 'National

Security' replaced all those categories of confidentiality, which simplified matters. You knew you stood no chance if charged with breaching an official secret.

Among hard core Complete Nigerian bureaucrats however, the reformation engineered by *The Nigerian Factor* has not swept way old usages. Words have merely taken on new meanings:

URGENT — 'make haste slowly.'

CONFIDENTIAL — 'Ssh! not so loud!'

SECRET — 'Don't tell it on the mountain.'

TOP SECRET — 'For your mistress's eyes only.'

B.U. — 'Bugger-U'. In other words, forget it. Your matter will not be brought up until you have become history.

The Complete Nigerian civil servant is so friendly he is eager to show you all the floors of the building where he works. This is done in a very subtle manner.

Let us say you have arrived to obtain Form PX which you require for permission to build a thatched hut for your ageing aunt, on a piece of land recently bequeathed to you by a dead uncle. You quickly discover that civil service bureaucracy is a minefield of barriers, route diversions and circumlocutory jargons, all of

"Form what?"

them designed to delay the man in a hurry.

You also learn very fast that lower down the ladder, public servants are monosyllabic.

The gatekeeper is the first to initiate you.

'To where?' he asks stopping you firmly.

The receptionist to whom he directs you is not interested in who you are.

'From where?' she asks instead.

The messenger is equally adamant that you shall not easily pass.

'Who you?' he demands.

The receptionist instructs you to go to Room 102, on the ground floor. But the man in Room 102 is peeling an orange and has never heard of Form PX. He suggests you go back to the receptionist and receive new instructions. The receptionist glowers at you because she has made a mistake on your account, corrects herself and sends you to Room 406, on the fourth floor, where you are told that the man you want is in Room 504, on the fifth floor. But of course when you get there, you are told the man who supplies the forms is off sick, and that he took with him the keys to the cupboard in which they are kept.

His colleague who imparts this sad news to you is extremely sympathetic, and after weighing your predicament for a while he makes an original suggestion, an idea that would never have occurred to you! 'Come back tomorrow.'

Tomorrow is another day. The gatekeeper recognizes you and honours you with a title: 'Chief,' he greets you warmly, 'morning.' His new respect reciprocates the ten naira you placed in his hand when you said goodbye the previous day.

The receptionist also knows who you are.

On your first visit, she made you fill out a form. It was a test of your mental ability. It asked you to name yourself, to state the time of day, the date, your address, the official with whom you wish to do business and the reason you picked on him. It also requested you to provide your autograph.

You noticed that when you handed back the completed document, the receptionist put it aside and forgot about it. It seemed it was unnecessary after all, but a standard bureaucratic procedure was satisfied.

'Alhaji,' she now says smilingly when you stand before her the following morning. The twenty naira you donated into her purse on your way out the day before has had a galvanizing effect on your relationship. You are now so completely in her favour when she learns you did not obtain the forms on your earlier visit, she loses her temper altogether and embarks on a voluble tirade against the failings of her bureaucratic colleagues. Even you feel she has gone too far when she threatens she would clear the whole lot out, if she had the power.

Meanwhile, a ragged line of twenty visitors has snaked into a figure vaguely resembling the letter 'Z', which is the shape of a patient Nigerian queue. They are waiting for the receptionist to finish her performance and attend to them. You donate another twenty naira to her kitty, to commemorate her support.

By the time you are at last in possession of Form PX, you have fully memorized the floor plans of the human anthill. Then you are told it is not Form PX you require.

It turns out that the inheritance from your uncle is designated farmland and that you are not permitted to erect a residential shanty on it. Furthermore, you need form PV, to regularize your possession of the property.

But you are a Complete Nigerian immersed in *The Nigerian Factor*. You know that every bureaucratic regulation is subject to avoidance, if you have the right connections. To achieve the trick of a residential property on designated farmland therefore, you procure the collaboration of a Complete Nigerian bureaucrat in whose safe hands you deposit what we in Nigeria delicately call a 'dash.'

The 'dash' is not strictly a bribe. It is a service charge for services rendered by a minor official doing his job. It is a negotiated donation demanded by a recipient with an undertone of vice in the proceedings. A 'dash' is meek gratitude expressed in cash. It is more often exacted by lesser bureaucrats as well as junior professional assistants such as traffic wardens, police constables, doormen, clerical staff, nurses, soldiers manning road-blocks, and out of work thieves with a credible patter.

The dash is in such demand that your tailor might even ask it in return for a promise to speed up work on the dress you plan to wear to your son's wedding.

A friend of mine visiting from Cologne purchased a beautiful hand-woven basket that was the envy of everyone. His travelling companions immediately placed orders for more. The Complete Nigerian weaver was not altogether keen. He asked for a dash.

Why, asked the Germans predictably, trying to discover the logic.

'*Massa*, one basket, no problem,' said the weaver, 'but twelve basket' — he shook his head from side to side, 'plenty work.'

A bribe, on the other hand, is a fee, not a service charge. In its more common form, it is a commission. In its more subtle state, it is represented by an over-invoiced icing on a contract-award cake.

A bribe is a dirty honorarium paid to motivate man of calibre and timbre who has the calibre to make timbre among the right calibres!

A 'dash' is a minor bribe; a bribe is a major 'dash'

Where is *The Nigerian Factor* in all this?

Answer: a man in a position to demand and receive a 'dash' but who refuses to do so is a dangerous man. A man who retires from high office but visibly lives within the means of his official income is stupid. It is an offence against the doctrines of *The Nigerian Factor* to live a standard of existence appropriate to the financial means of your office. Always live beyond the means. This shows you are clever.

The Complete Nigerian bureaucrat is a gentleman — at the right price. If you look after him he will kill for you.. But beware of imitations; fakes abound.

* * * * * * * * *

How to recognize a charlatan:

If he says, 'I cannot ask you for anything. You are my *Oga*.'

He means: 'I won't name my price, because I may undersell myself.'

If he says, 'Life is hard.'

He means, 'You can afford it.'

If he says, 'I know that if one day I come to you and tell you I'm hungry you will help me.'

He means, 'I won't demand anything now, but one of these days I'll turn up on your doorstep and you'd better remember you owe me one.'

If he says, 'What can I do to help?'

He means, 'I know what I can do to help, but I'm holding out for the right price.'

If he says, 'It depends on my boss.'

He means, 'There are at least two of us to share out the boodle.'

If he suddenly reverts to Pidgin English and says, *Oga* you know what they say, "Money na hand, back na ground," take your money and run. The man is uncouth and his palm is not worth the grease.

The phoney you must pray never to encounter is the radical Complete Nigerian civil servant who begins every sentence with, 'When I was in Europe. . .' or, 'During my stay in

America. . .' before he goes on to lecture you about the iniquities of corruption in the Nigerian society.

Give this Complete Nigerian a uniform and he thinks he is Napoleon; give him a desk as well and you have created a little Caesar. This type of bureaucrat has been highly successful during periods of military interregnum in our country.

Before he dismisses you from his presence he will ask you, 'What are you going to do about your corrupt politicians?' And then he will consult his 18-carat gold bracelet Swiss-made wrist-watch that cost 4,250 times his annual salary in naira.

He will excuse himself because he is running late for lunch in a swish restaurant where the three-course meal costs his monthly pay two times over.

The Waiting Game

IF you are a journalist who writes under a pen name, you meet more than your fair share of friendly Complete Nigerian bureaucrats. From them you learn that the length of time you are kept waiting to see a Complete Nigerian bureaucrat is directly proportional to the status of the official. The higher up the ladder the longer you must wait!

First, you encounter the Complete Nigerian messenger. He's reading a week-old daily newspaper when you arrive at his corridor office.

'My name is Peter Enahoro, I have an appointment with the Director-General'.

You can tell at once that this is not a man who normally rises to visitors with alacrity.

'Your name?' he says, meaning you have not spoken clearly the first time.

'Peter Enahoro.'

'From where?'

He speaks in a lugubrious tone half-way between incivility and private gloom.

'From London.'

'From London? All the way from London?'

You are exotic. You are from a far place. Mention of the metropolis cheers him into admiration. A star is born and you are that star. He takes a closer look at you and there is a shine in his eyes.

'Sah, I think I know you before. Are you not that Peter Pan, the one who used to write in the paper? Long time, sah. How's London? I'm so glad to know you today. I have been wanting to know you for a very long time since. Wonderful. . . How's the family? So, you come to visit us? Nigeria has changed, welcome, sah! Wonderful. . . You want to see the D.G., wait here small. He is in. I will tell Madam. Wonderful . . . Peter Pan!'

You are almost glad Madam is not at all impressed. She is the D.-G.'s secretary and a power in the land in her own right. She is also the D.-G.'s one-woman protection squad who is determined that the big man should not see people he has made an appointment with, without first consulting her.

She is a queenly matriarch dressed in a chic cocktail party dress at 10.15 in the morning. She is also wearing a frown.

'Madam, this is the man who has an appointment to see *Oga*.' Thus the messenger. Then in a stage whisper, 'You know him?'

The heavy madam is preoccupied, however, and says grumpily, 'Samson, where's the file I asked you to bring from Accounts?'

Samson, the effusive messenger, leaps to his own defence.

'Madam, I put it in the IN tray.'

'Did I ask you to put in a tray?'

Samson steps forward, takes out the offending file from the 'IN' tray and places it on the secretary's desk. Then satisfied that he has performed a bureaucratic miracle, he steps back and bravely introduces the matter of your appointment with the D.-G.

'Good morning,' says the secretary ignoring Samson.

'Morning.'

'Can I help you?'

'He wants to see *Oga*,' Samson enters a contribution in his self-appointed role of your public relations consultant.

'Do you have an appointment?'

'Yes; for 10.15.'

The majestic lady confers with her desk diary.

'You are Mr. . .?'

'Peter Pan!'

Samson it is who answers, but a glance from Madam shuts him up.

'Mr Enahoro, your appointment is for 10.15' Madam reads out from the diary. 'The D.-G.' she adds urgently, 'has a visitor. Please take a seat.'

Samson smiles conspiratorially. 'I think *massa* will see you,' he confides.

Madam dials a number.

'Sorry I had to cut you off,' she says into the mouthpiece. 'The silly messenger has not stopped interrupting me all day. As I was saying, you have to make up your mind. If he can't leave his wife, the least he can do even though you are

not married to him, is pay his own daughter's school fees. You can't do everything for him. After all, you have your own life to live. . . Hello, hello. . . Your boss? He's going out? How's he these days. . .? I know. (Laughs) Don't mind him. (Loud and prolonged laughter). Well, the next time he says that, tell him to buy me a car. Hold on . . . it's my boss. The light's flashing. I must go. Okay, I'll see you tomorrow. Yes, at Olaide's engagement party. Don't forget to wear the dress we bought together at Allen Avenue, with the matching shoes from Apapa. I'll be wearing mine. Yes, we'll knock them dead. I really must go. There's no peace in this office!'

She goes in to see her boss and you have time to ruminate on the adversities of life. You ponder whether there can be anything more daunting than an appointment to see a D.-G.

When are you likely see the D.-G.? Are you ever likely to see the D.-G.? Will the D.-G. remember he has an appointment with you? Does the D.-G. know you exist? Do you exist? Does the D.-G. exist? Is the D.-G. still alive?

'He will see you soon,' the secretary reassures you when she returns from his office.

Madam summons Samson for instructions: 'Make tea for the D.-G. and his visitor.'

Shall I make one for the *Oga* here?' asks the ever thoughtful Samson.

'Does he want tea?' Madam asks non-committally.

'Sah, tea?' Thus Samson to you.

Why didn't the British take the infernal habit of tea drinking with them when they left these shores? I can't see the point of drinking warm water poured over dried leaves and laced with sugar, in a tropical climate. Left to me our bureaucracy would abolish this inherited ritual which has withstood The Nigerian Factor.

You refuse the tea and you unequivocally dismiss the coffee. You only drink coffee to cure a hangover, which is why you've never really understood its taste. Right now it is the long wait to see the D.-G. that is killing you, not a hangover.

The trouble is you cannot even go for a walk. You may be forgotten altogether.

In the meantime, the D.-G. is invaded by a steady flow of lesser giants of the Ministry. They have all been briefed by the messenger in the corridor, and they stop to shake your hand, to pay you compliments, to ask you what you think of Nigeria; to seek your opinion about world affairs, recall old times, predict the years ahead, hope to see you again soon -- and then they disappear, and not one of them offers to break down the door to the D.-G.'s sanctum which is rapidly becoming a madhouse judging by the laughter emanating therefrom.

In spite of yourself you eventually lose your cool.

'Madam, I think you should remind the D.-G. I'm still waiting.' Madam is unmoved. In fact the sourness on her face is intensified. 'How long more must I wait?' you plough on nonetheless.

'I've told him you're here,' is all she says.

Your fears that the D.-G. may not exist are laid to rest, however. The great bureaucrat emerges from his office and leads out his guest. He sees the fellow to the door amid much laughter between them.

You have missed the camaraderie of the continuous laughter that echoed all morning in his office, while you sat waiting to see him. Now that you are face to face with him you find that a D.-G. is only a human being after all.

You had asked yourself, are D.-G.s made or are they born?

You even allowed a little prayer to form in your head, 'Please God, if it is true that there is reincarnation, next time I'm on this planet can I be a D.-G. so that I too can enjoy the privilege of keeping visitors waiting?'

The D.G. rouses you from your reverie and you instantly learn that a D.-G. is born, not made. His charm is infinite!

'Peter Pan, I'm so sorry to have kept you waiting. I had an unexpected visitor. I hope my secretary has been looking after you. Want some tea, or d'you prefer coffee?'

'No tea or coffee, thanks.'

'Make him tea, it's good for him,' orders the D.-G. with a burst of laughter.

Such friendliness.

If you see a man waving a tea-cup above his head, running helter-skelter through the corridors of a Ministry, and shouting, 'Where's the D.-G.? Where's the D.-G.?' do not think it is a mere storm in a tea-cup.

Restrain me!

11

The Taxi Driver

EVERY nation should be blessed with amiable lunatics. We in Nigeria are lucky to have the Complete Nigerian taxi driver.

He fills our lives with wonderment, with excitement, with senselessness and with danger.

What it is that incites a perfectly normal human being to become a Complete Nigerian taxi driver has never been fully explained. Indeed, this was the subject of a generously endowed research programme several years ago. Alas, the exercise was inconclusive. For, half way in its six-month schedule, the project was abandoned owing to the ludicrously high turnover in personnel.

The first group of researchers was recruited from Albania which was the most austere and rigid of all the East European Communist dictatorships. It was thought that the cruel discipline

they endured at home would give them a balanc-
ed view of the free-wheeling imbecility of the
Nigerian taxi driver.

But after only two weeks of riding in Nigerian
taxis, the two Albanian professors asked for
compassionate leave and flew back to Tirana.
There they died peacefully in their sleep within
twenty-four hours of their return. Doctors
reported that the sharp change to blessed peace
from the terror of accompanying Nigerian taxi
drivers on their runs was so acute that the sheer
bliss of the sudden restfulness killed them.

The Albanians were succeeded by three
hardened Egyptian traffic wardens who were
plucked from the unsafeties of walking the streets
of Cairo.

In the Egyptian capital, everyone drives in the
middle of the road astride opposite lanes. They
drive at great speeds aiming their vehicles at one
another. Then just when you think there's going
to be a horrific head-on collision, the cars swerve
violently away barely avoiding a smash-up.
Which can be disappointing if you have never
seen a great disaster and it had always been your
ambition to witness a spectacular car accident.

Such then was the civilization from which the
Egyptian traffic wardens came.

The third Friday after their arrival, they attended prayers as usual at the Central Mosque in Kano and no-one who saw them could have suspected anything unusual in their behaviour. But that afternoon all three took off and defected to Israel.

They set out on foot heading for the Sahara Desert, taking a route previously untrekked by man. They sent a note to the Egyptian Embassy explaining that they preferred to die in the desert. As for defecting to the enemy, they asked for forgiveness but prayed that their action should be seen as patriotic. They said that the compelling alternative was to embark upon the serial murders of Nigerian taxi drivers, which would have soured relations with the brotherly people of Nigeria.

A third and final group of foreign researchers was delivered from Rome, where taxi drivers dare pedestrians to cross the street.

Pregnant women have been known to give birth and celebrate the baptism of their babies while waiting to cross busy streets in Rome. You can age waiting to cross the square at the Emmanuel II Monument. I myself celebrated two consecutive birthdays while waiting with my wife to cross the square, to visit the little window from which Benito Mussolini used to shout to adoring fanatics. We finally made it when His

Holiness the Pope sent a message of sympathy and the Italian motorists had to pause to receive the blessings of the papal emissary.

Two men and a woman, all of good Roman stock, who together held the world record for standing longest on the pavement while waiting for a break in the traffic in order to cross a street, were brought to Nigeria and deployed to Ibadan, Kano and Onitsha. It took a mere five weeks for Nigerian taxi drivers to finish off the men.

The snoopers returned to Italy in distress. The recklessness of Nigerian taxi drivers made them swear so often they lost their nerves. As good Catholics, they were mortified by the frequency with which they invoked the name of the Devil; and so, as a penance, they joined an order of monks hidden in the mountain region of Sicily, where they were protected by the Mafia and where the only means of transportation was by oxen.

The woman would have gladly served her full term, but the Italian Embassy begged the Nigerian Government to deport her after she took to roaming the streets of Onitsha telling everyone she was a taxi and offering free rides.

The programme was eventually scrapped when a conference of Nigerian professors drawn

142

from all the universities was asked to select a body to undertake the research, but not a soul volunteered for the exciting venture.

An attempt to draft the conference chairman and members of the national executive was shelved when the chairman asked earnestly, 'Do you think I'm a mad man to ride in a Nigerian taxi all day?' Delegates agreed that only a mad professor would do so.

It is not surprising that after these unsuccessful attempts to unravel the mind of the Nigerian taxi driver, malicious rumours took over. They have persisted to this day.

It is said that the Nigerian taxi driver has brain surgery at the start of his career. The operation is carried out at a secret clinic headed by crazed herbalists who fortify their patients with the talismans that every self-respecting Nigerian taxi driver ought to carry on his person.

The herbalists have located the brain cells which control ordinary human intelligence. These cells are deliberately deadened and replaced with silicone chips through a process of osmosis infused by rubbing a magical ointment on the forehead.

This is what gives the Nigerian taxi driver his exclusive powers of observation and it explains why he does not view an ordinary road or its traffic situation with the same level of understanding as the rest of us mortals.

In fact, the taxi driver's vision is so far ahead of our times he is already driving in the Twenty-second Century when all Nigerian taxi-cabs will touch the ground only because they have to take on board or disembark, passengers; otherwise, to park for the night.

Our taxi-cabs of the future will be vehicles cruising at low altitudes. You can see why the Nigerian taxi driver of our age, with his eye on the future, is already driving at speeds that will surely take him into space one of these days.

These are the slanders the rumour mongers would have us believe.

Actually the Nigerian taxi driver is not a beast. He is even humble.

There was the case of a taxi driver who ran his cab into the rear of the presidential State limousine when Alhaji Aliyu Shehu Shagari was our First Citizen. One end of the tail lights was smashed into smithereens. Needless to say the taxi driver did not panic.

Gathering his wits about him, the cabman threw himself down flat on the ground before the large presidential automobile.

'Let no-one plead for me,' he remonstrated with the impassive crowd of on-lookers. 'Kill me. I insist. There must be no mercy for me. Even if you took me slave and tried to sell me in today's market, my price could not pay for the damage. So what can we do? I say kill me. Kill me this instant.'

The rogue was begging the presidential super chauffeur, who was alone in the car at the time, to kill him, with such earnestness, some women onlookers began to weep.

More penitence you could not ask for.

'No, no,' the taxi driver pleaded, 'do not beg for me. I'm lost!'

* * * * * * * * *

The Nigerian taxi driver is a felon, do not be mistaken. He is a cheeky cheat who will cheerfully over-charge a passenger he recognizes as a stranger in his town. He is a menace. At heart he is a road-hogging juvenile with the safety sense of a teenage joyrider. He is a devil of a tease who will not give a hand-signal unless he has completed the manoeuvre for which the signal was required.

He operates at two speed levels: stop, and go. In between he has the horn for elegant motoring.

'Go' is when the foot is on the speed pedal; 'stop' is that awful moment when he disembarks a passenger right there in front of your car, without a forewarning (Watch out for the limp left arm he puts out as an afterthought).

Despite all this, however, the taxi driver is a national institution, and I rather suspect the real reason we routinely want to beat him up is because we are all failed taxi drivers.

* * * * * * * * *

Most Nigerian motorists drive like the taxi driver, but though all men are born equal, all men are not equally talented. Thus it is that many a Nigerian motorist is a poor cut off the master himself.

Top of the imitation rankings is the man behind the wheel of that most celebrated public transport appropriately named the 'mauler,' better known in its Yoruba-English form as *molue*.

The *molue* driver is a charming bonehead who sometimes gives the impression of a psychopath. He shouts at other motorists; he is rude to his passengers; he throws tantrums at the conductor, who you will recognize as the man sitting half-in, half-out of the open doorway of a *molue*.

146

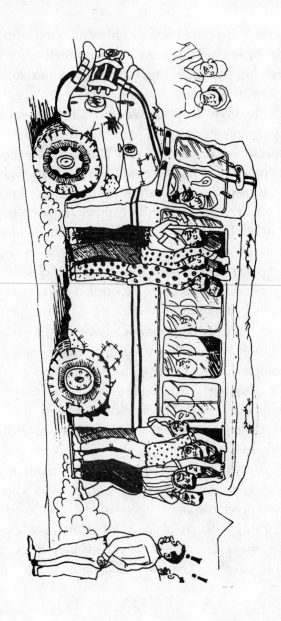

But despite his brutish facade the *molue* driver is a considerate professional determined to get his passengers to their destinations in one piece, if necessary.

He drives a contraption specially fitted for ferrying commuters. His mini-bus has undergone a special body re-work and attended a technical refit before being commissioned to ply its trade.

Boxers arrogantly show off their broken nose; the war veteran proudly exposes the scars of his battlefield wounds. The *molue* is dignified by its multiple dents.

A *molue* that wants to show class must therefore be taken to a breaker's yard where skilled panel beaters will give it a thorough going over with sledge-hammers.

In order that the vehicle may never come to a complete stop when kerb-crawling and touting for passengers, the brakes should be tampered with, to reduce their efficiency and thus to guarantee speedier mobility in the competition for passengers.

Among other 'extras,' you may remove the rear lights. Everyday is not Christmas so why do you need coloured lights in the rear of your *molue?* Also, re-shape the fenders by disfiguring them in such a way that they stick out obstrusively. This will endanger cyclists and teach them not to compete for space with your *molue* on urban highways. Lastly, replace all four new tyres with worn remoulds. Why use up good tyres when war is likely to break out in the year 2092 and the world will be faced with a serious crisis of tyre shortage?

But whatever you do, whatever you take out or put into your toughened *molue*, never ever mess with the horn. It is the most important mechanical device in a vehicle of any make or description for all Nigerian motorists of any group, age, sex or expertise.

Foreigners never quite understand just how important the horn is to the Nigerian motorist.

A Russian college professor seconded to Lagos University learned to drive in Nigeria. He passed his test at the first try and everyone remarked how well he adapted so quickly to driving in Lagos. Two years later, he returned to Moscow on leave and casually asked to borrow his brother-in-law's car. He wanted to show off his skills at the wheel.

As he told it himself to his Nigerian colleagues on his return to Lagos, he gave back the car in disgust after he'd been stopped four times in seven days, for bad driving. And this was a man who'd never once been asked to show his papers in Lagos!

'They just didn't understand me when I used the horn!' he said disdainfully.

For the sake of international accord therefore, here are tips on when to use the car horn in Nigeria.

• When you start the car for the first time in the morning, rev-up the engines by pumping the accelerator repeatedly to create an alarming roar and alert the neighbourhood you are about to leave home for the battlefields of the roads. Then when you are satisfied that the engines are properly fired and ready to go, sound the horn.

There is no technical reason for this, but it gives you a good feeling.

• Your children will come to the door to say, 'Bye, bye Papa.' You reply by sounding the horn.

• As you pull out of your compound gates or your garage, sound the horn.

• Toot the horn if you spot a neighbour's car waiting to join the traffic lane. This does not mean you are giving him permission to enter the traffic. It simply means, 'good-morning.'

If he's a gentleman he will sound his horn in return. Which shows that the horn is good for generating friendships. There is, however, a variation to this.

You may feel inclined to allow him take his

place ahead of you. In that case, sound the horn to let him know.

He will express his thanks by sounding his horn.

Meanwhile, behind you, several vehicles are sounding their horns impatiently, because your courtesy is holding them up; whereupon, you must sound your horn to tell them to go hell.

- Sound the horn before overtaking.
- Sound the horn when overtaking.
- Sound the horn after successfully overtaking.
- Sound the horn to show your fury if it is your car that has been overtaken.
- Sound the horn to warn pedestrians you are approaching, especially in urban places where they clearly see you. Then sound the horn to dissuade them from crossing.
- Sound the horn if you are displeased with other vehicles in the vicinity of your path.

For example, you may sight a car just about to start on a side road. There is a remote chance it may pull out before you have passed. Sound the horn to tell its driver not to attempt suicide, because you have no plans to slow down.

- Sound the horn once more as you go past. This means the car can now start its journey with your blessing.

- Sound the horn as you arrive at the office; sound the horn as you leave the office.
- Sound the horn as you enter a parking lot; sound the horn as you leave a parking lot.
- Other places where you may blow your horn are: expressways; political party rallies; before and after weddings; and any other occasions which make you happy.
- Sound the horn at the end of the day when you return home and the children crowd around the vehicle singing, 'Welcome, Papa.' Be sure they want to hear that horn blow. You have survived another day of car horn pandemoniums and they are thankful for it.

It may seem to the uninitiated that Nigerians sound their car horns at all times of the day and night. This is not so. There is more than one time when you may not sound your car horn. Here are the two occasions:

- Do not attempt to sound your car horn if the car's battery has been taken out. It will not function and you will be frustrated.
- Do not sound the horn if you are driving a stolen car. Car theft is rampant in Nigeria and you have nothing to bray about.

Footnote

I AM the designer of a remote control device that will permit a car owner to sound his car horn from his bed, to say goodnight: but I have failed to obtain a patent.

The official reason for the refusal is that it cannot be guaranteed not to interfere with the tumult of police escort vehicles which accompany our many VIPs on their fast rides through traffic jams, and empty roads. Their sirens raise the most tremendous rackets, however, and I cannot imagine that any human device can silence them. Therefore, it is my considered view that at the root of the refusal is pure, unadulterated jealousy.

I had made it clear I would not market my invention and the idea that a lone Nigerian among all our population would hold a monopoly right to blow the final horn of the day was too much for envious officialdom to bear.

Finally...

My Ugandan friend, Mbitiru Oyek, who was Idi Amin's secret guru on Human Rights suggested three highly original solutions to the problems of reckless driving in Nigeria:

(a) impose a mandatory IQ test for all professional drivers. Every professional driver should be able to identify the trafficator lever and be bright enough to explain why he does not use it;

(b) remove the horn from all motor vehicles;

(c) amputate the left arm of a professional driver before giving him a licence to operate a taxi-cab or *molue.*

Mbitiru Oyek was always a gentle soul.

12

Sex and The Complete Nigerian

A popular play ran for years on the British stage. Its title:

'No Sex Please, we're British!'

The poor things.

Yes, sex please; we're Nigerians!

Is this a myth? Hardly.

In the Western world they say they marry for love.

Vive la difference!

In our world we marry for more.

It remains a tradition in rural Nigeria that the Complete Nigerian marries for the same reason a farmer gathers cows around his bull. As in so many things urban corruption has intruded to distort this working arrangement. Once marriage was an orgy of masculinity, but an institution for female virtue. Not any longer. In civilised Nigeria marriage is a union between a husband's restricted bacherlorhood and a wife's amorous discretions. This is because the Complete Nigerian male has a big heart. He can always find a place in it for more than one woman at a time.

For the new Nigerian woman love is what you have when you are having an affair; marriage is an assignment.

Convention says that only a woman can commit an act of infidelity. All that an unfaithful husband has done is sow wild oats.

Thus a Nigerian magistrate once said, "Illegitimacy is a European concept."

If a monogamously married Complete Nigerian retains a mistress everyone will respect the relationship, as long as the woman herself respects the liaison by rigidly staying above suspicion. She will be praised as a woman of exemplary discipline and high morality.

Should she bestow her favours on another man, however, she will be denounced as an adulterer; a woman of weak character. And if the man did not cease to pay court to her immediately his image would be stigmatized with harlotry. For the difference between morality and debauchery is in the mistress's loyalty; not in the marital status of the male partner, but in the macho firmness with which he dominates the affair.

Among the peoples of the so-called developed world they talk incessantly about sex. They even photograph their women in explicit, skimpy apparel. Their classiest women show their legs all the way up provocatively slit skirts; enough at any rate to satisfy curiosity.

When a famous television star was caught by the tabloid Press breast-feeding her baby the entire British male population had orgasms for a week. When she was subsequently photographed curvaciously modelling shorts that would have caused a stampede in Nigeria the Britons merely said, 'nice.'

In the down-to earth world of the Complete Nigerian a scantily dressed woman scandalizes herself by the brevity of her skirt and not by the cleavage of her blouse.

Vive la différence!

Whereas the Western European youth is traumatised into early and high sexual expectations by romantic novels and soppy melodramas in woman's magazines, the young Complete Nigerian is told that sex is for grown-ups to experience.

He grows up with the wisdom of an old bull and zest of its young seed.

A Nigerian bull and his young offspring so the story goes, stood on a promontory looking down upon a spread of cows in the valley below.

"Father," said the young bull 'lets gallop downhill and take a couple of cows each.'

'No, my son,' said the old bull wisely, 'let's walk down slowly and take them all.'

Observe how in accordance with the uncompromising directness of the Complete Nigerian scion the old sod did not bother to instruct the young stud on the merits of foreplay. Only on the need to conserve energy.

Vive la différence!

13

The Common Tongue

A self-made Complete Nigerian tycoon whose businesses took him all over the world was on the telephone to the new English secretary at his London office. His call had come through in the middle of a raging monsoon thunderstorm in New Delhi and Lisa the secretary was not doing too well trying to decipher his words at the other end of the line.

'Chief, did you say, "Long gone " Who's long gone?'

'No, no, no!' the great entrepreneur snarled into the mouthpiece. 'London! You don't hear, "London?" I spell it for you: *Elli* for elephant, *Oh* for knottin', *Any* for nought, *Dee* for dem. . .

And that is the trouble with the English language. You can spell it perfectly correctly and still offer no sense.

The fact is that the English language is no

longer English. It is our official *lingua franca*, the most widely-spoken vernacular in Nigeria. It is also our only patriotic vehicle of communication.

One of our more showy military regimes flaunted its patriotism when it peremptorily abolished the National Anthem of our First Republic. It was offensive, it said, that the national hymn was composed by a foreigner.

The highly jingoistic super regulators consequently supplied us instead with a flag-waving dance number which only makes sense when sung in the English language. Thus although it hurt our pride that our National Anthem was written for us by a foreigner, it has not troubled us one bit that we can only sing its successor in a borrowed mother-tongue!

Several years ago, no less an authority than His Excellency, the Nigerian Ambassador to Bonn put the Germans in their place over the matter of our devotion to the English Language.

Our man had accepted to lend his dignity to the annual get-together of the German-Nigerian Friendship Society. As befitting a Complete Nigerian of his status, the envoy saw fit to arrive late. Being a man of considerable modesty, however, he refused to be ushered to his allotted place on the podium. It has to be said, however, that he demurred the offer in so loud a voice that the rafters shook. Furthermore, all coyness was quickly discarded when it struck our man that the German on his feet was speaking in German!

Our ambassador put his hand up.

Mr Chairman,' he thundered from the back rows, 'I want to remind the speaker that this is the Nigerian-German Friendship Society. Therefore, he should speak in English.'

So there it was.

A foreigner who wishes to establish a rapport with the Complete Nigerian had better learn to speak English.

Despite its complete absorbtion into our national heritage, however, the English language continues to present problems entirely of its own kind.

The Irishman playwright George Bernard Shaw, from whose works generations of Englishmen have learned to write their own language properly, observed that 'it is impossible for an Englishman to open his mouth without making another Englishman hate or despise him.' He could have said it of the Complete Nigerian.

Just recently two Complete Nigerians were arraigned before a magistrate on a charge of causing a minor affray. His Worship demanded to know why two grown men would exchange blows in a public place.

The pompous lawyer of one of the defendants rose to explain.

'With respect, your Worship,' he said stiffly, 'the argument was over an English word.'

'Proceed,' said the magistrate equally primly.

'Well, Sir, my client had said something he thought would amuse the second accused. Instead the second accused took offence. My client is from Akwa-Ibom state. By way of explanation he told the second accused that what he had said was meant as a "yoke". All of a sudden the second accused fell about laughing. My client realized at once that the second accused was laughing at him because of the way he pronounced the word "joke".

'Well, Sir, a friend of theirs happened to be on the scene. He asked the second accused what was so funny. The second accused, still convulsed with laughter, pointed a finger at my client and said, "He say yoke instead of zoke." The second accused, I should point out, is from Edo State.'

'Where is the witness now?' asked His Worship,

'He's gone to None-done,' said the prosecuting police sergeant helpfully.

162

'Gone to where?'

'London, Sir,' said the defence counsel. 'The prosecutor is from Delta State, Sir.'

From the back of the courtroom came a piercing hiss, followed by an oath.

'I show you phefa!' a disembodied voice intoned.

'Order!' the magistrate barked. 'What was that?'

'Someone is threatening to show somebody pepper, Sir,' the court orderly called out.

'Pepper? I thought I heard "phefa".'

'Yes, your Worship. But he's from Kano State.'

'I will have order in this court!' rasped the magistrate. 'I must remind you that here justice is instant. This not a shursh.'

'Did I hear the magistrate say shursh?' the reporter of the *Daily Truth* asked his neighbour in the Press gallery.

'He meant church. He is Ijebu from Ogun State.'

'Open the window, let climate come in,' said Inspector Ozouwe to the nearest usher, trying to suppress a laugh.

This was overheard throughout the courtroom which instantly became filled with laughter!

Experts are predicting that by the middle of

the Twenty-first Century Complete Nigerians shall require pocket computers if they are to understand one another. For it has emerged that English as she is spoken has evolved its own special boundaries in our country.

One of our most famous radio sports commentators once excitedly told his listeners, 'Well the match has ended in a one-one goalless draw!'

Postcript

AN announcement on the notice-board of one of our plushest hotels directed guests to the location of a major annual event thus:

POLICE OFFICERS WIVES ASS
Dancing
Banquet Hall
No doubt a great view was had by all.

14

The Complete Nigerian Abroad

SOMETHING colossal and fearsome happens to the Complete Nigerian the moment he sets foot on foreign soil.

He becomes a patriot, a monster, a freedom fighter, a bully, a big spender.

Unscrupulous, tetchy, wildly funny and utterly unreliable, the Complete Nigerian Abroad is an enigma and a bundle of contradictions. He is an interesting bloke to meet.

Millions of Ordinary Nigerians live perfectly unremarkable lives abroad, many in decently paid professions. They are law-abiding, show admirable initiatives and run successful businesses. They are the envy of other African population groups who think that every successful Nigerian abroad is linked to a secret pipeline through which his government feeds him oil-money.

As you can imagine, these Nigerians are boring. Honesty is the best policy but it doesn't make good reading.

The Complete Nigerian Abroad is the big noise. You will recognize him immediately. His charm is overbearing. His voice is loud and authoritarian, especially when he is on the defensive. His attention to the bureaucratic requirements of the host country is sloppy, and he tries to cover it with an off-putting gregariousness. He relishes his personal rights and rates them higher than any law. His abiding wish is that the world would do things his way.

The Complete Nigerian Abroad came into his own during the oil boom years, as an offspring of the promiscuous petro-dollar fertility which swept Nigeria into an orgy of spend, spend, spend!

Suddenly there were thousands and thousands of Complete Nigerians Abroad swirling like locusts, with more money to spend than the wisdom of what to buy with it.

First, let us lament the demise of that Innocent Complete Nigerian Abroad, the newly rich businessman journeying overseas for the first time to join and rub shoulders with that breed of

167

international entrepreneurs known to the popular press as 'oil-rich'.

He was parented by a thing called 'the quota system', and his birth certificate was issued on an import licence. We should never forget him.

He passed away with the advent of maturity and experience.

I have in my possession a dossier on an Innocent Complete Nigerian Abroad of that period who interrupted a business visit to Czechoslovakia with a stop-over in Italy, to savour a night of Roman hospitality.

He formed an association with a car hire firm chauffeur called Luigi who showed him the sights and sounds of Rome and had him carried away by a temptress called Sophia.

The next morning, the newly oil-rich Complete Nigerian returned early to a deserted Rome airport having bid the Senorina Sophia *ciao* at an unconventional hour.

Our Innocent Complete Nigerian Abroad dumped his suitcase and sat down at the first Alitalia desk he found, just as Luigi had instructed. Then tired out by the night's events he slipped into a much-welcome coma, though this was not part of the Luigi plan.

Several hours later he woke, stretched himself and studied his surroundings. There was nobody behind the Alitalia desk before him, but further down the hall other desks were busy attending to queues of passengers. And so, more out of curiosity than for reasons of a special nature, our newly oil-rich Innocent Complete Nigerian Abroad joined the nearest queue.

'Sir, your flight left an hour ago,' he was told when it came to his turn at the top of the queue.

'What you mean?' asked our newly oil-rich Innocent Complete Nigerian Abroad genuinely baffled.

There was something about his tone which failed to assist the mood of the desk clerk, however.

'I mean gone; finished,' said the Italian fellow flapping his arms like a bird in flight.

This was different from what Luigi had said would happen. Luigi had told our Innocent Nigerian Abroad that he should settle down in front of any Alitalia desk and that when the staff came they would check him through. Luigi, an Italian, had told him this; and he had done exactly as he had been advised to do.

'Is this Alitalia desk?' he asked.

'You don't understand. . .' the clerk began to say, but the Innocent Complete Nigerian Abroad was having none of it.

'No, you don't understand. I want go for

Prague. I have ticket. What you mean "gone", "finished"? Now you find me another aeroplane, because I come here this morning even before you wake up in your own house. You think I come late? You think this is first time I fly aeroplane?'

'Sir,' said the Italian abruptly, 'you are holding up the queue.'

'Shut up!' shouted the Complete Nigerian.

Italian airlines ground staff, like Italian policemen, are a match any day for any grouchy, newly oil-rich Complete Nigerian Abroad.

'Next, please,' the Italian called over the shoulder of the oil-rich Innocent Complete Nigerian Abroad, in what should be said was a rather unruly fashion.

Apart from the fact that this behaviour did not go any where near enough towards appeasing his temper, the real matter of getting our Innocent Nigerian Abroad to Prague did not appear to feature on the desk clerk's agenda.

The Complete Nigerian made a fist and rammed it on the desk.

'You think I am a small boy?' he queried. 'I tell you I must go Prague and you tell me "next"!

The queue had become restless, with several

170

passengers muttering discontent in a variety of international languages. By way of apology for blocking any further check-in, the Innocent Complete Nigerian Abroad turned to face the queue and narrated his story.

The previous day, he explained, the girl at the transit lounge had told him it was alright to break his journey in Rome.

She had said and he remembered this clearly: 'Tomorrow you come back and you go to Alitalia.' Luigi, an Italian friend, had told him the same thing: go to Alitalia. That was precisely what he had done. But the Alitalia people were late and now they were trying to cover up their own incompetence by telling him he had missed his aeroplane!

As he concluded his evidence before the jury of impatient passengers, the Complete Nigerian spotted a Black figure hurrying past. The Innocent Complete Nigerian Abroad hailed him.

'*Psst. Psst.* My friend, please.'

The Black man went over to him.

'You Nigerian?' the Innocent Complete Nigerian Abroad asked him.

'No, Zambian.'

'Same thing,' said the Innocent Complete Nigerian wearily. 'You speak Italian?'

'No, only English.'

'Me too. You see, this people here they no understand English. Only this one,' he added sweeping a contemptuous gaze in the direction of the clerk. 'What kind people be this no understand English, tell me. So, anyway. . .'

He retold his story in its entirety, concluding with the plea, 'Help me tell this man, maybe he hear you better. If I no go Prague today, I beat him here. *Allah!*'

That night the Zambian eye-witness told his experiences to a group of us in Cologne, in return for several rounds of rum-and-coke which he said he needed to help ease the memory of the encounter with a most unusual oil-rich entrepreneur.

Nigeria bred hundreds of these romantic figures at the height of the oil-boom years in the Seventies; but, alas, they disappeared quickly, leaving the stage to be occupied by the remaining clans: The One-man Conglomerate; the Container load Tycoons, and the baby of them all, the Society of Invisible Haberdashers.

The One-man Conglomerate

NO Nigerian of any physical size, skin colour or tribal facial marks has made such an impact across the length and breadth of the globe as the one-man conglomerate known, admired and disparaged as 'The Nigerian Businessman.'

The Complete Nigerian Businessman Abroad has done oodles to strike fear into the hearts of foreign smart-alecs, such as passport control officers, travel agents, hoteliers and car hire firm operators who would otherwise take the Nigerian for granted. All the intimidations duly registered by the Ordinary Nigerian Abroad among would-be foreign business partners is down to the entrepreneurship of the Complete Nigerian Businessman Abroad.

He mixes pleasure so much with business he is a fine specimen of the Ugly Nigerian.

He packs a mean line in self-promotion. He is flamboyant and apparently lives year-round in hotel suites, which he runs like railway stations with guests arriving and departing all hours of the day and far into the night.

He rarely sleeps alone. His late night companions include permanent and non-permanent, resident and non-resident, girlfriends.

Sometimes, however, he is hard up for entertainment and you have to sympathize with him. These are the times when he brings the wife along to compensate her for her dignity at the recent christening of his latest child born outside wedlock.

He thinks an overdraft is a congratulatory message from his bank manager. He is a high achiever.

At the zenith of his powers he is a braggart, a pushy, coarse, lavish spendthrift. He has a tendency to flit from one unfinished business obligation to another, in search of a further quick-kill. He is the distortion whose scandalous image has influenced the foreign perception of the Nigerian business partner.

At home, however, his contacts are impeccable. He is a conscientious operator whose sleeping business partners are powerhouses in the corridors of power.

Every trip abroad is an odyssey that begins at the domestic international airport.

He arrives with just a few minutes to spare so that his arrival at the departure lounge makes a maximum impact. He expects to be recognized by all and sundry, including the girl at the check-in counter.

He alights from his car and personally supervises the removal of his cases because he knows which ones he will advise the airline to weigh-in and which others he will cheekily refuse to have weighed.

He forms a one-man procession to the check-in counter, waving to airport attendants who know him, and stopping to greet security staff who remember the last handshake with him from the naira note that get stuck in the palm after he withdrew his hand.

'Chief, are you travelling again?' one of them asks, deliberately at the top of his voice, so that attention is drawn to the traveller. Despite his frequent sojourns overseas it makes his day when everyone is reminded that he is a frequent flier.

'I'm afraid so,' he sighs. Then in a voice befitting a public rally, he says, 'I'm off to Norway through Geneva and Stockholm.'

The boom echoes through the lounge, which is no mean feat as dozens of other Complete Nigerian Businessmen similarly heading for foreign climes are just as aggressively clamouring for attention.

The Container-load Tycoon

THE Container-load Tycoon is a merchant prince.

He buys, he sells; he buys and sells. And then he buys and sells again. Originality is not his strongest point.

He is an impudent copy-cat, the proprietor of a one-man industrial espionage network which lies in wait until someone else has introduced a new product into the Nigerian market from abroad and shown that it can be sold at a profit. Then the Container-load Tycoon will move in with a price seemingly made for charity, by undercutting the going market price.

The Container-load Tycoon is intellectually untenanted and makes no pretence about that. But do not hold him cheaply. He is loaded with cash.

The brilliance of his business acumen rests on a robust scent for ferreting out the current vogue in consumer cravings. Whatever it is that Nigerians are currently crazy for, he will go to any lengths to buy just so he can sell it to them.

'Na lace dey move now,' he would say and go out to bring a container-load of lace materials.

He has a hard nose for profit and an ingenuous flair for wheedling a deal out of you before you know what has hit you.

He is quick to pick up a smattering of the language in the foreign places to which the markets take him. But while overseas he will studiously maintain a low profile because he is socially insecure. At home, it is different; he has a taste for cheap night-clubs on whose dance floors he lurches and pitches like a robot out of control.

He is instantly recognizable by his mode of

176

dress. His favoured fashion are baggy trousers, held up by flashy braces popularized by a famous talk show host on American television, beamed into his home via a giant satellite dish occupying the entire garden space of the tenement block where he rents his rooms. Because the braces must be seen to be believed, the jacket is carried and never worn.

It was my pleasure recently to share a hotel lounge with a young couple who were obviously very much in love. I knew at once that he was a Container-load Tycoon becuse of the red, blue, purple, yellow and green flower-patterned braces. I knew also that he was a high flier of the genre because he wore the braces back to front. As they left his lady friend carried the jacket while our man strode two paces ahead of her displaying his polished Italian leather shoes. Sheer class!

A self-respecting Container-load Tycoon is sure to carry a wad of currency notes with him when invited to glimpse the life further up the social ladder. He will unload the lot on a girl at such a gathering in full view of everyone in order, he hopes, to buy himself a little respect. Otherwise, he believes that money is only good for buying and selling and buying and selling. . .

His entire filing cabinet is contained in the

attache-case that is always at his side. He is the chairman, managing director, chief accountant, chief cashier and chief security officer of a company with the legend, 'J.C. Bardoh and Sons International (Ltd.), Exports and Imports.'

J.C. Bardoh has no sons. To speak the truth, J.C. Bardoh does not even have children. He is young, virile and unmarried. He exports nothing. But 'J.C. Bardoh and Sons International (Ltd.) Exports and Imports,' is a stylish title to have for a company operating from the front room of a one-bedroom flat with a communal bathroom and toilet, and a shared kitchen.

In the First Republic the equivalent of the Container-load Tycoon was a figure labelled 'Aba Trader.' In the Second Republic, the Container-load Tycoon's predecessor invented the electronics import market and single-handedly deregulated import restrictions long before the International Monetary Fund hit upon the idea. During the Second Military Interregnum his fortunes rose and imports by the container-load became his trade mark.

It was his aunt Veronica Nyem-Mili who summed up the success of J.C. Bardoh, the typical Container-load Tycoon.

His cousin Hejanus Atilogu Mokwelu had

"The Tycoon!"

returned from studies in the United States with a doctorate degree in economics. The family was justifiably proud and Aunt Veronica led the public jubilation. She could not resist boasting to everyone's hearing.

'Now we have a doctor in the family, the Nkwere Odibo family will have to watch their step. For years they would not let me rest since that albino-type stutterer of theirs returned from I don't know where calling himself "doctor." Its been "doctor said this, doctor said that."'

'Auntie, I'm not that kind of doctor,' Atilogu intervened.

'Of course you are not, my son. You would never adulterate laxatives given to patients. Because of the charlatans we have these days a person now has to take several tablets just to break wind. In the old days they gave you a solid dose and they were so effective you were lucky to make it in time to the loo.'

Atilogu laughed. I mean, I'm not a doctor of medicine.'

'You are not a doctor?' Auntie Veronica asked looking puzzled.

'Yes, I am. I am a doctor who tells people how to make and manage money.' It was the nearest her nephew got to explaining 'economics' to her.

'You poor boy,' said Auntie Veronica sadly, 'you mean you went all the way to the White man's country to learn how to make money? Onitsha Market is full of Nnewi people who know how to make money and they haven't even crossed the River Niger! As for looking after money, how do you think the Obosi people got to where they are? Container-loads, my son, full of spare parts! From that place they call Taiwaney. Ask your cousin J.C. He deals in Container-load. God forgive my mouth,' she said crossing herself, he learnt it from his father, Obosi man! He hasn't been further than Lagos and look at him. Your poor father. . . spending all that money. Better not let those loud-mouthed Nkwere Odibo hear this.'

Auntie Veronica's eyes were moist as she picked up her handbag and went inside the house to commiserate with her brother.

Because the Container-load Tycoon operates mostly on the quiet he should not be confused with that black sheep of his clan — the Emperor Cocaine.

The Society of Invisible Haberdashers

THE under-class Complete Nigerian Business Person Abroad is the super-woman who scours the small high streets of the lesser known European fashion centres to bring home the gaudy trinkets and other bijou so highly fancied by the Nigerian woman.

She is one of that unquantifiable breed of indefatigable Nigerian business women who travel frequently abroad so unobstrusively as to be virtually invisible. She owns a small outlet but mostly she operates out of masses of suitcases containing the wares she has imported by the trunk-load.

She is brave, adventurous and strangely loyal to a shameless husband or lover. She is often the provider in a one-parent family; otherwise, she is the work-horse sent out to earn the extra funding for the comforts of a stud who presides over a multiple-wives domestic arrangement.

Invariably barely literate she, however, possesses an encyclopaedic knowledge of Europe's open markets where she can save that extra tiny, naira, so that back home she can make that extra, tiny, profit. Her bargaining skills are legendary, as many an exhausted leather goods merchant in Genoa, or the Belgian lace manufacturer in Brugge, not to mention the London cabman, have found in their time.

She shuns posh hotels. Indeed, she shuns all hotels. She prefers the cosy intimacy of a doss

182

down on a sofa in the living room of an accom-
modating acquaintance. Once in a while she may
splash out on a lodging house, but she would
sooner sleep in a railway station or the airport
lounge, if only the busy-body policemen abroad,
would let her.

She carries a quantity of home-cooked meals
with her on her forays into foreign lands where
the food is lousy, such as in France!

The Nearly Forgotten

AN astonishing number of Complete Nigerians
choose to live abroad permanently. They must
be distinguished from the Ordinary Nigerian
Abroad who either has never been or has ceased
to be a Complete Nigerian.

The Nearly Forgotten Complete Nigerian
Abroad does not live in ghettos. On the con-
trary. He does not even go out of his way to
identify with other Nigerians. He has no sense of
permanence abroad however, and talks incessantly, almost obsessively, of 'when I return
home.' Or, he says things like, 'When I was in
Nigeria. . .' He keeps pushing any real plans for
his return to Nigeria away from his mind. He is
his native land's greatest critic and bombards Or-

dinary Nigerians Abroad with fanciful rumours. He is the one with the latest authoritative news from home!

'Nigeria,' he will say shaking his head, 'what are we going to do about our country?' Then he will quote at great length from the columns of a local newspaper whose reports of Nigeria are scanty and selectively sensationalist! Otherwise, he will fill you in with correspondence from relatives all of whom want to join him overseas and who in their letters to him paint the most gloomy pictures of life in Nigeria.

'You cannot imagine how bad things are. . . yet another supplicant has written. Based on this flimsy evidence our Nearly Forgotten Complete Nigerian Abroad tells the first Ordinary Nigerian Abroad he meets:

'Those Nigerians. . . your people: they're killing each other again!'

Nigerians are 'your people' when the news is bad.

His attitude to Nigeria is ambivalent. For instance, he is not a nationalist, but he will not permit a non-Nigerian to make a disparaging remark about his country. When surrounded by nationals of his host country he will wilfully create and nourish a romantic nostalgia about Nigeria which contradicts his private opinion.

Most Nearly Forgotten Complete Nigerians Abroad will never return home.

They are found in unexpected places in Africa, the Caribbean, Europe and Asia. But they congregate mostly in the United States of America.

There they are distinguished by their American slangs spoken in Nigerian-English accents spiced with the enunciations of Jewish refugees from Minsk in Russia.

They are living proof that human ingenuity is truly remarkable. When they gather in one place the Nearly Forgotten Complete Nigerians Abroad in America, are actually able to understand what one of them is saying to another.

I have been witness to this extraordinary communication, having spent an entire evening at a reception in my honour during which I did not understand a word of what was said to me. I knew, however, that the speeches were about me because successive speakers smiled at me and occasionally I recognized my name when someone said, 'Enero' which is not a long mile from Enahoro.

They were kind, generous and overwhelmingly eager to please. But to my untrained ear their accents rendered the conversations as intelligible as when the Hallelujah Chorus is sung in reverse.

Footnote

Three Extraordinary Nigerians

During the twenty-five years of my self-imposed exile I was privileged to meet an array of extraordinary Complete Nigerians Abroad. I learned from them that abroad' is a funny place filled with funny people Also, that in an emergency there is no wittier, more spontaneous improviser than a Complete Nigerian. He becomes a consummate actor, he tells fabulous lies and he extudes a blinding charm.

The Consummate Actor

The most accomplished performance I know of by a Complete Nigerian in a spot of bother abroad took place on the Austrian-German border.

A Complete Nigerian on a business trip to Austria decided on the spur of the moment to visit a cousin in Bremen, Germany. He knew the Germans would not issue him a visa in Vienna. They would insist that he returned to Lagos to apply for it.

The Complete Nigerian hired a car nevertheless and headed for the border. He was dressed to kill in flowing Nigerian robes and counted on his charm to see him through.

But the Germans are not famous for their inflexible compliance with regulations for nothing. He ran straight into a stone wall of German bureaucracy.

Two sphinx-like border guards studied his passport with the briefest peep into its pages and told him coldly, 'No visa. You cannot Germany come into.'

The Complete Nigerian broke down in tears.

'Please, I beg you,' he said making a piteous spectacle of himself. 'It is my brother. I have not seen him in years and our mother is old. In Africa, if I return and I do not tell her I've seen him . . . well, it will be . . .' He drew an invisible line across his throat with a forefinger, 'It will be good night to me forever.'

Then the grown man, a father of four daughters, fell to his knees and wept bitterly.

He next rose to his feet and lifted first, the right leg, then the left leg, then again the right leg; just as he had seen American Indians perform on the screen in Westerns. It looked like a ritual dance.

Suddenly our resourceful Complete Nigerian

poured out a torrent of Yoruba vernacular pleading earnestly for understanding.

The Germans backed away in alarm. They'd never seen or heard anything like it; if it came to that, they'd never seen anything quite so disgraceful either. For our Complete Nigerian was now prostrate at their feet, blubbering.

'Sango! Sango oh, baba ina . . .'' he intoned like a common witchdoctor a-la Hollywood.

'Do you think he's gone mad?' the first German asked the other.

'You can't tell the difference. They are imbeciles ordinarily,' said the other.

'This one seems a chief the way he's dressed.'

'Do you think he's an important person?'

'It's possible.'

Our Complete Nigerian was back on his feet executing another jig.

'What is he doing now? the thicker of the two guards asked. 'When they dance they are dangerous. I saw it in a film. . .'

'Better let him in. He's got a return ticket and he's been in Germany before.'

'Yes, several times,' confirmed the German holding the passport.

Our Complete Nigerian drove through the border and laughed all the way to Bremen. It had not occurred to the guards to ask him if he

188

understood a word of German, which he spoke perfectly adequately.

The Terrible Liar

It serves the Europeans right that they are ready to believe the worst about Africa. In particular, I have no sympathy for the British.

I happened to be at London's Gatwick Airport to meet a flight from Lagos. On the flight was Aina, the girl friend of a friend's friend. Oseni, a Complete Nigerian Abroad, also a friend of the friend, had come to meet her too.

We were returning to his car struggling with the half-dozen suitcases Aina had brought with her for her two-week visit when Oseni noticed suspicious activities around his car.

Four men were circling the car making preparations to tow it away. A mechanical arm already stood poised to lift the vehicle off the ground.

'Hey!' Oseni called out breaking into a trot. 'Officer . . . that's my car!'

'Is this your vehicle, sir?' the policeman directing the operations asked unnecessarily in that inimitably dead-pan fashion of the British cop.

'I was away only ten minutes,' Oseni lied.

'And that, sir, was ten minutes too long,' the cop replied drily.

My fellow countryman threw up his arms in a gesture of despair.

'I'm tired,' he said resting his weight on the door of the car.

He looked so sad and so completely fagged out it seemed he was about to collapse. Even the men preparing to tow away his car hesitated in their task.

'This is the worst day of my life,' the Complete Nigerian moaned. 'Over there,' he said, holding out a weak arm towards Aina, 'is my sister. She is terminally ill. She can hardly walk. Aids,' he added quietly. 'Raped by soldiers five years ago. They came back this year. She has just escaped a massacre in our village and trekked through the jungle. Three days without food or water. My mother . . . the news is bad. My brothers are missing . . .'

'Are you Biafran?' one of the handlers, a little Asian fellow asked.

The Nigerian civil war had ended several years before, and Biafra had long ceased to hold world attention. Obviously the Asian had not heard the news. Oseni refused to spare him. 'Yes,' he lied, 'My whole village has taken to the bush. Some White missionaries helped my sister to get away.'

'You've had problems then, sir?' the

policeman commented rather sympathetically.

'Problems?' the Complete Nigerian shook his head. 'I should be dead!'

'All over Africa is trouble,' said the Asian, 'Same thing in Uganda. I am coming from Uganda where I am living twenty years and Idi Amin is coming and spoiling beautiful country. Your sister, she is looking so tired . . .'

Everyone turned in Aina's direction. Her slender figure was leaning on the trolley, and you could tell she was irritable with jet-lag. Her boy friend had told her Oseni knew his way around London and was versed in the ways of the British people. 'He will take good care of you,' he had told her. Now she was despondent and it showed. What she was witnessing was not her idea of a man who knew his way around London, she thought. In Ibadan, where she knew her way, and where men were men. Oseni would have long settled the matter of his car with a cash-induced handshake with the policeman.

Look at her,' Oseni said. 'Three days trekking the jungle. An aids victim for that matter. She's finished . . .'

I have to admit that Aina was more thin than slender.

'How long have you lived here, sir?" asked the policeman.

'A few years.'

'Then you do know you shouldn't have parked here?'

'It was silly of me. It's my nerves. I just wasn't thinking. Sorry, officer.'

'Terrible things in Africa. They are killing all the time.' The Asian was almost beside himself. 'Every day I am saying to my wife, thank God we are leaving Uganda long ago . . .'

'Will you move the car now, sir?' the policeman said. 'I should have the young lady see a doctor at once.'

'Harley Street,' said the Complete Nigerian without elaboration.

He came back to Aina smiling mischievously. 'I know these people,' he boasted. 'They think they're clever!'

'You were lucky,' I said.

'Give over. Did you think I'd let them tow away my machine? I'm a Nigerian. I know my rights!'

The Charmer

A PLAYMATE from my days of high-spirited carousals in Lagos undertook an elaborate detour through Europe just to spend an evening with me in Brussels. For days I looked forward eagerly to

192

the reunion. Then we met at Brussels Central Station and I wanted to die.

My old soul mate had become a successful businessman and was accordingly bedecked as befitted a successful Complete Nigerian businessman.

The full set of Nigerian robes in new wool was loudly embroidered with gold thread. A long gold chain hung from the neck to the knees, and a twenty-two carat solid gold name-bracelet weighed heavily on his wrist. If all this was predictable for a successful Complete Nigerian Businessman Abroad, he carried things a bit far with the polo-neck jumper, the ski-slope shirt and the knitted sweater he wore underneath the flowing robes. True, it was winter, but Brussels is not Siberia and he looked a sight.

I once told the story of an unfortunate incident involving two Nigerians who had not met for some time. One fateful afternoon while shopping on a busy London high street, they sighted each other and shouted recognition.

Their embrace — actually it was a crashing crush — occurred in the middle of the street as the two Nigerians enveloped themselves in mutual bear-hugs dancing and cheerfully throwing playful punches in a fullsome Nigerian greeting. A dour British policeman more accustomed to the monosyllabic cough-drops by which an Englishman would have drained his emotions on a similar occasion thought the Nigerians were fighting, arrested them, and took them into custody allegedly for disturbing the Monarch's peace.

Nothing of the kind happened as my visitor came at me. His billowing outer garment became accidentally attached to a trolley as he rushed to me. I was frantically endeavouring to warn him, but he mistook my hand signals and continued to sail towards me. The handcart caught his leg, tripped him and threw him off balance. All four tons of my mighty friend cascaded on me.

'Peter!' he whooped and, bang! I swear all the lights at the station went out at that very instant. It was blink and out! *Kaput.*

I am not a physicist, not even an electrician; but I swear the superior power discharged by my visitor caused those lights to go out.

'Just like Nigeria,' he called out merrily referring to the power cut. 'Or, is it me?' he added jokingly.

I said nothing. At any rate I could hardly speak at that very moment. I was suffocating inside the folds of his robes among which I had disappeared as he took me into what was meant to be an embrace.

Mercifully I heard him say, 'Let me see your face! Is this your eye?'

'Unless you release me,' I said choking, 'I can't tell you about the eye. As for the face, the last time I saw it in the mirror which was this afternoon, I can say, yes, it is mine.'

My friend laughed so uproariously window panes rattled around us.

'The same old Peter!' he said approvingly and struck me a blow in the nape of the neck by way of affection.

When I came back to life I noticed that an on-looking crowd had formed around us. Several good-natured Belgians were flashing their teeth at us, nodding approval of our forthright salutation.

A stout old lady carrying several shopping bags entered the circle. She seemed a nice person.

'Lumumba!' she shouted at us. 'Lumumba!'

That was all she said and then she was gone.

I thought she was trying to say 'hello' to us in 'African,' but it seemed more likely she was telling us to clear-off.

My old pal was a seasoned traveller and as a Complete Nigerian he had not bothered to make a hotel reservation. However, he was dead set on a five-star establishment in the heart of the city.

'Don't worry, they know me there, ' he assured me.

They didn't. But my friend was not a jot put off.

'How's your manager?' he asked breezily.

'Sir?' said the starchy receptionist none too co-operatively.

My friend was sizzling with the effervescence of a man very much at home:

'Your manager. The tall one. With a moustache. Dark hair. Very nice man.'

'You don't mean Mr. McWinter, d'you sir? He's not very tall and he doesn't grow a moustache.'

'Maybe he's changed. Anyway, he knows me. I always stay here when I'm in Brussels. I like the way you look after your regular guests. I was here last year and Mr Karton . . . there! That's his name. Karton!

The receptionist hesitated.

'Sadly, Mr Karton has left us,' he sniffed.

'He has resigned?' My man's surprise was spoken so loudly a waiter dropped a tea-cup. 'Why? Where's he now?' he demanded to know.

The demeanour of the receptionist indicated that he was not prepared to impart further information about Mr. Karton or his whereabout.

'Well sir, it's a long story,' he said evasively.

My pal whispered into my ear, 'What he's just said is European for embezzlement. I can tell. There was something fishy about that man. Turning to the waiter, he said, 'So, have you got my suite?' This was said so sudddenly, so unexpectedly, so completely out of tune with the run of the conversation and with such confidence it threw the receptionist off-guard. 'I'd like the same suite I had last time,' added my friend for good measure.

The confidence drained from the clerk, but he was not about to give up without a fight. He knew he was before a master, a man who could be playful one minute and a bully the next, but he was trained to deal with men like this.

'Do you have a reservation, sir?' he asked.

It was now the turn of my old chum to summon his reserve strategy.

'Not at all,' he replied unhesitatingly. The way he said it you knew he meant that precautionary manoeuvres of that kind were below his dignity.

All cordiality terminated at that point. The receptionist said there was no suite available. My pal said there had to be. He said he was personally known to all the hotel chain's managers

197

..ork, London and
.......hung Lee had even told
him to mention his name every time he booked
into one of the chain's establishment anywhere in
the world. So, what, my friend demanded to
know, was this nonsense about a suite not being
available?'

The desk clerk assumed an arrogant attitude.
Nothing seemed to impress him, not even when
my friend reeled off the names of all the best
hotels in the world where he could walk in and
obtain a suite at the snap of a finger.

But let's face it, there is a limit to human en-
durance and as such there is a cut-off point after
which even the most haughty desk clerk in the
plushest hotel has to give way to the sort of bar-
rage of credentials with which my visitor was
harassing the man under review.

'There is a slim chance,' the clerk quivered at
last, beginning to waver. 'A slim chance . . . a
guest who's overdue . . .'

My Complete Nigerian did't give him another
chance.

'Overdue?' he barked, 'He's late! He has only himself to blame. What's my room number?'

He got the suite.

On our way up in the lift, he said to me, proud as a peacock, 'That's how to be a Nigerian!'

"Haven't you got any Rice?"

And he hit me flush between the shoulder blades. I was still seeing stars as I sank gratefuly into a chair in his suite.

*   *   *   *   *   *   *   *   *

Two years later, the same old buddy came to visit me in the little village where I lived outside Cologne. He had despatched a cable from Lagos barely twelve hours before setting off and his warning did not reach me until well after his visit. At any rate, I was away when he arrived.

A neighbour found him sitting on a suitcase outside my door. Fortunately my neighbour knew I was due back that day and invited him into his flat to await my return.

My Complete Nigerian accepted the invitation with alacrity. He made himself so completely at home he took off his shoes and rested his tired feet on the coffee table.

That was for starters.

Bye and bye, my neighbour asked him, 'Would you like a little something to drink?'

'Whisky,' said my friend bluntly, not being one to beat about the bush with niceties like, 'Yes, thank you, I could do with a spot of something.'

200

Whisky was duly served.

Much later still, my neighbour asked his increasingly drowsy visitor, 'Would you like a snack?"

'Oh, yes.'

Tea or coffee?'

'Haven't you got any rice?" the Complete Nigerian demanded with a straightforwardness so rare in good people these days. 'I'm hungry.'

Tea was served, with sandwiches. And then because these were despatched so quickly, scones were served. They went down equally quickly. The remnant of a celebration cake that Inge, my neighbour's wife had kept for the forthcoming visit of an aunt was reluctantly brought out to nosh-up the alimentary carnage.

After a ninth cup of tea to wash down the enormous smorgasbord of replenishments, the visitor leaned back deeply in the couch, gave off a deep yawn, and went to sleep.

'It would have been wiser if in the first place we had boiled some rice just as he asked,' said Inge ruefully afterwards. 'He was very hungry.'

There was a touching ending to the story.

Two months after he returned home, a large package arrived for Inge and her husband. The postmark showed it came from Lagos. Inside it were two gorgeous hand-made leather cushions of the finest quality.

My Complete Nigerian had not forgotten their generosity.

The accompanying note said simply, 'To two wonderful people who filled my stomach when it was empty. On day when you visit me in Nigeria I shall take my revenge.'

I became a legend in Quadrath-Ichendorf. I had done nothing to deserve it, but I became the celebrity whose friend took off his shoes, rested his feet on Inge's coffee table and asked for rice.

The *Burgermeister* told the story at the village council meeting. The village *polizist* officially reported the matter to headquarters in Cologne. The *priester* used it to illustrate his sermon, citing the precedent of the Biblical Good Samaritan.

In the tiny village supermarket, I had tears in my eyes when mothers pointed me out to their tiny tots: *Dar ist der Neger* whose *freund* put his feet on *Tante* Inge's coffee table.

Turkish immigrant workers stopped to shake my hand in the streets.

Every time I went into the *wirtschaft* total strangers paid for my drink and then proceeded to tell the story to complete strangers.

As a result Quadrath-Ichendorf gained a reputation as a place where you got a free drink just for stopping by the village pub to hear the

202

story of a Black man who came and rested his feet on Inge's coffee table.

I thought things were getting out of hand when the village council requested the German Tourist Bureau to include Quadrath-Ichendorf on the recommended list of local places of interest to American G.I.s, based in the next-door village of Kerpen. A photograph of the block of flats where I lived was sent, with the suggested legend: 'Here lives the African whose friend . . .etc.'

I finally fled Quadrath-Ichendorf when I received the information that plans were afoot to commission a statue of me for the village square.

I didn't know it then, but I was on the first leg of what proved to be a protracted return journey from self-exile.

End